An Old Negro Spiritual

IN PROSE

BEING

A Haint Story of Injustice

BY

MARCUS MCGEE

PEGASUS BOOKS
Copyright © 2021 Marcus McGee
All Rights Reserved

Copyright © 2021 by Marcus McGee

All Rights Reserved. No part of this book may be produced or transmitted in any form or by any means, electronic or mechanical, including photocopying, recording or by an information storage and retrieval system—except by a reviewer who may quote brief passages in a review to be printed in a magazine or newspaper—without permission in writing from the publisher.

Pegasus Books
8165 Valley Green Drive
Sacramento, CA 95820
www.pegasusbooks.net

First Edition: January 2021
Published in North America by Pegasus Books. For information, please contact Pegasus Books c/o Marcus McGee, 8165 Valley Green Drive, Sacramento, CA 95823.

Library of Congress Cataloguing-In-Publication Data
Marcus McGee
An Old Negro Spiritual/Marcus McGee– 1st ed
p. cm.
Library of Congress Control Number: 2020952557
ISBN – 978-1-941859-83-4

1. LITERARY COLLECTIONS / American / African American. 2. PHILOSOPHY / Ethics & Moral Philosophy. 3. POLITICAL SCIENCE / American Government / Judicial Branch. 4. HISTORY / African American. 5. EDUCATION / Urban. 6. RELIGION / Christian Living / Social Issues. 7. FICTION / African American / Christian.

10 9 8 7 6 5 4 3 2 1

Comments about *An Old Negro Spiritual* and requests for additional copies, book club rates and author speaking appearances may be addressed to Marcus McGee or Pegasus Books c/ Marcus McGee, 8165 Valley Green Drive, Sacramento, CA 95823., or you can send your comments and requests via e-mail to mmcgee@pegasusbooks.net.

Also available as an eBook from Internet retailers and from Pegasus Books

Printed in the United States of America

PREFACE

I have endeavored in this Spiritual little book, to raise the Haint of an Idea, which shall not put my readers out of humor with themselves, with each other, with these troubled times, or with me. May it *haint* their houses unpleasantly, and no one wish to experience it.

Their faithful Friend and Servant,

M.M., or M.H.

December 2020

Contents

Shout I
Marshall's Haint

Shout II
The First of the Three Haints

Shout III
The Second of the Three Haints

Shout IV
The Last of the Haints

Shout V
And That's That

FOREWORD

There appears to be a proliferation of Black authors in recent years. In keeping with Black History Month, I would like to highlight—no—put an asterisk next to a Black author whose his name is Marcus McGee, the author of *An Old Negro Spiritual*.

A January 2021 release, this well-researched and artfully crafted novel by Mr. McGee starts with the dawning of the Emancipation, and it is chocked with detailed histories and insights that continue up through the Civil Rights Movement before proceeding to modern times.

This cautionary tale is shared for the benefit of its protagonist, Judge Dolittle, a Supreme Court Justice. It is an enlightening and enjoyable read!

Dr. Gregory E. Douglas

An Old Negro Spiritual

SHOUT I

SHOUT I
Marshall's Haint

Marshall was dead, to be sure. There was no debating that. After a long and distinguished life, both as a lawyer and judge, he had died in a Bethesda hospital bed with a nation looking on. His coffin was displayed in the Great Hall of the Court, and the funeral took place in the National Cathedral. Dolittle attended the funeral, detached and deferential, as he and the old man hadn't much in common. Old Marshall was gone indeed, but not forgotten.

Ah, but I must make a distinction here, as there is a difference between one having been forgotten versus never having been known at all. Generations had been born and had grown old in the time since Marshall made his name in Topeka and changed the way children went to school. Most of these children would scarce even recognize his name or realize how profoundly he had affected their lives, learning and attitudes. For that, he could never be forgotten.

Thomas Dolittle knew he was dead? Of course he did. How could it be otherwise? Dolittle was, after all, his legacy. Dolittle was his sole heir, his sole executor, his sole administrator, his sole assign and his sole residuary legatee. But Dolittle valued little his inheritance and cast aside Marshall's ideas of integration as a silver bullet, or even true equality in America, favoring instead those of an individualist and conservative rationale. Legacy aside, Dolittle never exhausted thought to truly *understand* Marshall.

Over time, Dolittle had never been able to blot out Marshall's name or obscure his memory, nor did he try. There it stood, years afterwards, high above the court-house door: Marshall, and then Dolittle. The legacy was known as Marshall and Dolittle, though it was an inarticulate legacy.

Sometimes people new to the business called Dolittle "Dolittle," and sometimes they called him "Marshall," but in frustration he answered to both names. It was all the same to him.

Oh! But Dolittle had a tight-fisted hand at the written opinion, whether favoring the majority or expressing dissent, Dolittle! a squeezing, wrenching, grasping, scraping, clutching, angry old sinner! Resentful, self-righteous, and stubborn, his mirror held no image or a cure. He was strong-willed, self-determined and revengeful, indignant as a child who felt abuse.

Ironically, the protests of his own people exaggerated his Hamitic features. They broadened his nose, darkened his skin, stiffened his gait; made his eyes jaundiced, his black lips thick and quiet-spoken, suppressing the Gullah rhyme ever present in his ears. They placed a kinky gray rime on his balding head, and on his eyebrows, and on his wiry, white-haired chin. He carried a flaming air of anger and resentment about him. He hardened his heart in warming spring and in the heat of summer, and he did not cool by one degree, come October.

While Dolittle was a respected judge, he was never well-liked, even from a child. The resentment he felt from his own people only made him more convinced of his duty to pursue a course to show those people the truth about race—for their own good. His stern grandfather, who raised him from a child, made him to realize that discipline was a sign of love, that punishment and condemnation was proof of love, and it imitated the example of God. In this mind, the judge who wanted better for a people mustn't *enable* those people.

Uproot entrenched ideas of impractical ideals! Refuse to enable them—for their *own* good! He didn't say it out loud, but he suggested as much on the rare occasions when he did speak. No, he was a man of few spoken words, rendered silent by childhood ridicule. He was doing the work of God, though "they could not understand." They taught him to hate racism and colorism, though not by their own examples or protests. He could not love those people, as he saw and experienced their hypocrisy first-hand. In the looking glass, he saw what they saw, though he *refused* to recognize the caste to which he had been assigned by their tortured self-definition.

He had learned to harden his heart and steel his face during encounters with *those people*, had deafened his ears to their arguments and criticisms. Oh, to him they were a difficult, bitter and resentful sort! Indisposed to fairness, hard work and education, overly animated, overly religious and often pompous, selfish, jealous, immoral, fractious, disrespectful and ignorant of the very principles they had been conditioned to exploit. *Save a tenth of them!*

None of them ever stopped him on the street or on an elevator to say, "My Dear Judge Thomas Dolittle, is it well with you today? When will you come around to see me?" No pleaders expected sympathy, empathy, understanding or goodwill from him. No children admired him or sought his guidance or advice or ever sought to follow in his plodding footsteps. None of their men and women once in all his life inquired advice or direction from Dolittle.

While the Dark Caucus over at the House appeared to know him, when they saw him coming on, they would urge their constituents not to listen to him, would urge them to oppose him and disregard him. They would seem to say to him and the country, "None of ours is better than *one* of ours who is blind and cannot see himself, or us!"

But what did Dolittle care! It was the very thing he liked. To edge his way along the crowded paths of life, warning all human sympathy to keep its distance, and those who knew him prayed that he would one day "come to Jesus."

Once upon a time (of all the good days in the year), on the eve of the birthday of the King history, old Dolittle sat busy in his courthouse chamber. It was cold, bleak, biting weather, with fog everywhere! He could hear those people outside the court, suffering under heavy weights and pressured from all sides, clamoring for fairness, justice and opportunity, and stomping their feet upon the pavement stones to sue for relief.

The city clocks had only just gone three, but it was quite dark already. It had not been light all day, and dim bulbs flared in the windows of the neighboring offices, like the final flickers from a fireplace, exhausted of fuel.

Fog and misinformation came pouring in at every chink and window and was so dense without, that although the court was narrow, the legislative buildings across the street seemed ghostly. It seemed the fog had merged with the low-hanging clouds, obscuring everything. It was a perfectly ominous day, a precursor that perhaps Nature was brewing dark things on a larger scale.

The door of Dolittle's courthouse chamber was open so that he could keep his eye on his Hebrew legal clerk, who in a dismal little office down the hall—a sort of cell—was writing his master's recent court opinion. Dolittle had a very small light, but the clerk's light was so very much smaller that it looked like a candle, barely flickering.

But the legal clerk couldn't modernize it or seek ongoing education, as Dolittle kept him to the narrowest interpretations and strictest rationales. He was Third Tier, after all. As surely as the clerk came in with the written dissent *to* dissent, the master predicted that the clerk's days were numbered in that office. It made no sense the clerk had hope for Dolittle and tried to warm him with ambitious ideas of unanimous opinions. More trusting than pragmatic, he failed.

"Justice and Equality, Uncle! And a little compassion, please!" cried a hopeful voice. It was the voice of Dolittle's nephew, Freddie, a man of the streets, who was scarce recognizable in bandages from a recent beating by the Law, salt-and-pepper dread locks hanging down his shoulders. "We'll have justice yet."

"Justice? Equality! That's *yunt*," said Dolittle. "You say that because you're a criminal, nephew."

"A people freed is all we need," Freddie preached. "No longer crime in that, indeed. Don't you know all the *doers* are punished, Uncle?"

He had so heated himself with constant protesting in the fog and frost—this injured nephew of Dolittle's—that he seemed hot, if not a little high on something.

His steaming body was muscular, and his face was handsome. His eyes sparkled as he breathed smoke again. Because he was such an articulate mouthpiece for the "other side," he was Dolittle's favorite nephew and foil, though the judge would never admit to it.

"We can't get any justice," Freddie complained.

"*Old man Can't is dead!*" Dolittle replied, "*I helped bury him.*"

"You've always told me that, but you've also told me that justice for us cripples and burdens *your* privilege?' Do you still think so, Uncle? 'Equality for *us* is a tax and unfairness to *you*?'" he asked. "I've read your opinions, but you can't *believe* them in your heart. I mean, seriously, Uncle?"

"I do," said Dolittle. "Justice and equality! What right have you to call for justice, or anyone? And for what reason do you speak of equality? You count yourself among the poor, those of lesser quality, when you are none of the sort. Those people you've adopted and their adopted problems matter none to anyone in the overall scheme."

"Negro, please!" returned the nephew, shaking his head, though with a proper degree of respect. "Whose idea was it to let *you* sit in judgment? And why do you diss your nephew, your family, your people? You're rich enough and married *buckra*, but you'll never be truly adopted by them *buckra*, and you know that in your heart!"

Dolittle, having no better answer ready on the spur of the moment, said, "You *yunt,* boy!"

"Aw, don't get your drawers all twisted," said the nephew. "It's all good."

"It is not all good! All will never be all good! How else should I be?" returned the uncle, "when I live in a world full of fools who never stop with this ridiculous justice and equality! And now reparations? For all these years, those people have preached *ad nauseam* for justice and equality. Society has grown tired of hearing it for 100 years!"

"Here's 200 more years of preachin and protestin if we have to!" the nephew said. *"Where there is no struggle, there is no progress."*

"What's equality to you but an entitlement to eat and to receive healing and other benefits without money?" Dolittle asked. "What is justice for you without class warfare and the redistribution of wealth through taxation and unnecessary regulation? To you, justice means getting you and your friends more free things?" the judge continued, "but it only makes you more dependent on your so-called 'oppressors'."

"You have earned a great many things, my uppity uncle," the nephew said. "You've even earned your cynicism, though you still don't get it. You're a Booker T-Rex, an elitist dinosaur!"

Dolittle grabbed his nephew's left arm and rolled up his sleeve, exposing the watch on his wrist.

"You, Nephew, pretend to be a protester, hiding a Rolex and who you really are. You scheme to exploit a nation's former sins," Dolittle answered, "abusing collective guilt and pity, rather than using your backs and minds in a good and productive work? If I could have my will," he said indignantly, "every idiot who goes about with 'justice and equality' on his lips should be taken out, strung up and whipped, and banned from public speaking out altogether. He should! And if he is shot in the streets, then so be it!"

"Like Ahmaud and George, Uncle?" pleaded his nephew. "Do you hear yourself?"

"Nephew!" returned the uncle, sternly, "Keep your justice in your own way, and let me keep it in mine."

"Keep it!" repeated Dolittle's nephew. "Please! And you think *you* keep it?"

"Let me leave it alone, then," said Dolittle. "Much good may it do you! What have you *ever* done with what was given you?"

"My father, who was your brother—he sent me to good schools," his nephew returned. "I have a comfortable enough life. If I had wanted to really get over in this world, I would have *been* done got over, but once we stop becoming a people because we're all selfish individualists, we've lost our souls. How can we not consider King's message on the day of his birth? All my life I've thought of him, in January, when there's a special day set aside to remember his legacy and the life of privilege he sacrificed for us."

"Sacrificed? You never knew him. When I was young, I admired him, but he *changed* over time and became damn unrecognizable!" Dolittle snapped. "He was good, but then he became something else!"

"Dead men don't change, Uncle," 40-something Freddie said. "The judgment and convictions of the living change as the intellect declines. Still, I've always encouraged folks to read and consider the words he spoke and wrote, to dream the dream he dreamt, not for a day, but for a whole month.

"It should be a time when we consider each other as men and women of goodwill, when we understand and support the struggle of the oppressed, when we work to open shut hearts and we think of people as they really are. On the most basic level, we're all headed to the same human grave, Uncle. We're not separate races of creatures, destined to unconnected outcomes."

"I admired King at one time too, but he was an ordinary man!"

"That he was, but more honest than most," the nephew said. "And therefore, Uncle, I believe honoring him is a good thing, and though it has never put a dollar in my pocket, I believe it will do me good. As I always say, 'It's all good!'"

"Speak the truth, my brotha!" blurted out the voice of the clerk in the next room, but acutely aware that the exhortation would not be taken well by his boss, he turned up the volume on his tablet and pretended to be listening to a religious sermon.

Un-fooled though not un-irritated, Dolittle hollered harshly to Heschel, the clerk, "Turn off that nonsense, man! And if I hear one more *Amen* from the choir pews out there, I will grant you all the freedom you want to *join* the struggle of the oppressed!"

"But Monday is the holiday to celebrate the birth of that King, Uncle," the nephew pivoted. Surely you'll close your office in his honor? You of all people!"

"Why him and why not me?" the judge sneered. "Am I not honorable then?"

"All honest men are yet honorable, though some not yet," answered Freddie. "Don't be a hater, Uncle. Come to Black Sunday Dinner tomorrow. We havin yo Daddy's gumbo, black-eye peas, collard greens, she-crab soup and red rice. You know they're your favorites. *Kum bah yah!* Come on *home*, Uncle."

"*Tie yuh mout, boy!*" Dolittle snapped. "They're not my favorites. They've never been my people! I'd rather wrestle a *boo hag*!"

"But I don't get it!" cried Dolittle's nephew. "Why?"

"Why? Why do you *care* about them?" asked Dolittle.

"Because they're our people."

"Because they're *your* people, not mine in my appointment!" growled Dolittle, as if that were the only one thing in the world more ridiculous than *equality and justice*. "Later for you, boy."

"Hold up, Uncle. You never came to Sunday Dinner *before* your appointment. Why give it as a reason for not coming now?"

"Go way," said Dolittle.

"Go way? What's wrong with you, Uncle? I ask nothing more than for you to get real, be authentic for once. Why can't we ever just share in generations, like all families should?"

"Go way," said Dolittle. "Get out!"

"I am sorry with all my heart to find you so hard. In my own way, *I* am your legacy, and I'll fight for justice and equality to the end. I would put my life on the line for that, for you to understand that. No justice, no peace, Uncle!"

"Go way!" snapped Dolittle.

"And power to the people!"

"Fo the lass time," Dolittle sighed, disgusted. "Go way, boy!"

His nephew left the room without an angry word. Notwithstanding, he stopped at the outer door to bestow the spirit of brotherhood on the clerk, who, cold as he was, was warmer than Dolittle as he returned the exhortation cordially.

"There's another fool," muttered Dolittle, who overheard them. "My clerk, making not much more than five hundred dollars a week—with a wife and family no less! To hear him talking about justice and equality!"

This lunatic, in letting Dolittle's nephew out, had let two other fools in. The first was a greasy, hefty man, a *brotha* who probably hadn't missed many meals; the other was a tiny, brown-skinned Hispanic woman with an accent who wasn't bad-looking, and the two stood in his lobby with presentation materials out. They already had the money collection computer app queued up on one of the tablets.

"Dolittle and Marshall's, I believe," said the black man, referring to his list. "My name is Will, and my colleague here is Esperanza."

"Good afternoon," she said, smiling. "Have we the honor, then, of meetin Judge Dolittle or Judge Marshall?"

"Have you two been asleep? Judge Marshall's been dead some twenty-seven years," Dolittle replied. "Yes, he died twenty-seven years ago, almost to this same week."

"Sorry to hear that, but we don't doubt his liberal *values* remain well-represented by his surviving partner," said Esperanza, presenting her card and credentials.

They certainly were not, since Marshall and Dolittle had been two un-kindred spirits. At the ominous word "liberal," Dolittle frowned, shook his head and handed the tablet back.

"During February, Judge Dolittle, we've set aside a month of recognition for our people," said Will, re-presenting the app, "we're encouraging those of us who have gotten over in the Man's system—those who are not unwilling subjects of the slave state, we're asking them to make some slight provision for the oppressed, slain and imprisoned, who are dealin with it these days. Many hundreds of thousands ain't got the necessities, thousands are killed in the streets by cops every year and other millions suffer in prisons and detention centers, sir."

"Are there not enough prisons then?" asked Dolittle.

"Too many prisons," Esperanza answered, re-presenting tablet with statistics. "Black and brown people make of 45% of the total U.S. population, but we're 65% of the prison population. Two and a half million black and brown people are locked up right now, sir, on this very day! We're incarcerated at 5.6 times the rate of whites."

"Because you'd rather steal things and sell drugs rather than work! What about jobs in the service industry?" demanded Dolittle while pushing the tablet away. "The country's unemployment rate was under 4% before Covid-19, and it'll go back there soon enough. Low paying jobs still are jobs, and they provide a decent living."

"Not quite, judge," returned Will, "Still, I wish I could say they did."

"And anti-discrimination regulations and minimum wage requirements are still the law of the land, as I remember?" challenged Dolittle.

"So far they still exist, sir."

"Oh! I was afraid from what you said at first that something unusual had occurred to stop them in their useful course," said Dolittle. "I'm very glad to hear it."

"They're the law of the land, but they sadly don't provide an even playing field for minorities and underprivileged whites or hopeful opportunities to the working class," returned Will. "That's why a few of us are endeavoring to raise a fund to provide for capital investment in underserved communities for business start-ups and expansion. We choose this time because it's a time, of all others, when wealth inequality abounds, when the top 1% owns 43% of the nation's wealth. You are in that top 1%. What shall I put down for your investment in our communities?"

"Nothing!" Dolittle replied.

"Okay... I take it, then, you want to be anonymous?"

"No, just leave me out of it," said Dolittle. "Since you ask me what I want, that is my answer. Nothing! I didn't get to where I am in life through affirmative action or white patronage, and I have no desire to make special provisions and give jobs and opportunities to unqualified candidates, no matter who they are or what color they are. I help to support the core establishments—law enforcement, the court system, the executive branch, and I pay my taxes, which cost me enough. They have welfare, Medicare and the ACA."

"Many can't get Medicare or ACA benefits. Thousands die unnecessarily each year."

"If they would rather die than go to work," said Dolittle, "then let them do it, and decrease the government-dependent population. Besides—excuse me—I don't *know* that."

"But you *should* know it," observed Esperanza. "You're a powerful judge with a *duty* to know these things."

"It's not my business," Dolittle returned. "It's enough for a man to understand his own business and not to interfere with other people's. Mine occupies me constantly. *And it really bugs me that someone will tell me, after I spent 20 years being educated, how I'm supposed to think.* Go way!"

Seeing clearly that it would be useless to pursue their point, the public solicitors withdrew. Dolittle resumed his work, a little full of himself, with even more attitude.

Meanwhile, the fog and darkness thickened, so that certain of those people ran about in crowds while marching with provocative placards, all the while shouting provocative phrases. "No Justice, No Peace," they declared, taking their places before cars, trucks, buses and trains in protest, inconveniencing the irritated masses, who sought to get on their way. *Oh, what foolishness!* Dolittle thought.

The Church and liberal organizations, which were once the citadels of justice and whose righteous indignation was always peeping slyly down at Dolittle from a place of moral authority, they had become invisible, barely audible, and seemed to fall in line for their own selfish and political purposes, much to their discredit. The threatening cold became colder still.

At Main street, at the corner of the court—the homeless, cold and ignored, had lit a great signal fire in a garbage can-fashioned brazier, round which a party of ragged, starving men, women and children were gathered: warming their hands and blinking their tear-swelled eyes before the blaze, disillusioned. All charity and goodwill abandoned, those at the city's margins became sullenly complacent and ceased to believe justice was even possible.

Blocks over, in the brightness of the marketplace, where the heat of corporate greed disguised the darker purpose of enterprise and the vanity of hard labor, they crackled in the lamp-heat of the windows, which made dark faces dusky as they passed. Small business, small farms and independent grocers became a splendid joke: they were propped up by government plans and subsidies that would cement their undoing. They knew it, but they were helpless to save themselves.

The Lord Governor, the country's leader, in the stronghold of the state's mansion, gave orders to his fifty sous-chefs and butlers to keep the oppressed in oppression—as a Lord Governor's household should do. Even his bankrupt political consultant, whom he had fined $200 on the previous Monday for speaking without authorization and being sympathetic to protesters and the press, he whipped tomorrow's talking points to dishonest media influencers.

The Lord Governor's un-original wife, with his children and pet projects set-up for free government money, toed the line and deceitfully acquired millions of dollars in CARES relief checks, PPP loans and block grant benefits.

Foggier yet, and colder! Piercing, searching, biting cold. Yet despite the bitter clime, there came a-singin and a-rappin three teenagers on the sidewalk in front of Dolittle's office. The first apparently had church training for his speech and a soulful voice, which fell on the judge's tone-deaf, stopped-up ears.

I was born by the river, in a little tent,
Oh, and just like the river, I been a-runnin every since.
It's been a lon-ong, a long time comin,
But I know-oh-ooh-oh, change gone come.
Oh, yes it will.

If the unrequested street spectacle, without a permit, wasn't enough to draw old Dolittle's ire, then the politically charged and extemporaneous expository/political hip-hop commentary from the rappers got an instant response. Dolitttle called the police, who, owing to his station, arrived not longer than one minute later.

"I want these boys arrested," Dolittle demanded, "on the grounds of trespass and disturbing my peace!"

"It's a public sidewalk, brotha!" the oldest of the youth complained. "Now I believe in bein peaceful, and courteous.

Obey the law, respect everyone, but if someone puts his hand on you, send him to the cemetery."

"Arrest them!" Dolittle insisted. "That violent uppity one just *disrespected* me and threatened me!"

"Judge Dolittle. You're a powerful man," one cop said, "but this *is* a public sidewalk, and we can't arrest this young man just because *you* say he disrespected you."

"Take his side, will you?" Dolittle threatened. "Either you arrest them, or I'll be addressing your dereliction of duty to your superiors."

"Arrest them for what?" the confused cop asked.

"Make up something! *A public concert without a permit!* It's easy. Look at them! They're black teenagers—they must be guilty of something! They probably have criminal records. You know what to do."

The second cop approached the boys, his voice implying a threat. "You boys got any ID?"

"I ain't no boy, boy!" Malcolm, the more aggressive young man snapped back. "Look, it's Black Sunday Dinner tomorrow, and then the King holiday. We ain't leavin and we ain't showin you no ID!"

"Then I have no choice but to arrest you," the second cop insisted, "for obstructing or delaying a police officer by not providing ID."

"I'm only 15," complained John, the youngest of the boys. "I ain't even old enough to have ID yet."

"Then why don't you guys just leave," the first officer said, "before this gets any worse."

"Well, *when you see something this is not right,*" the boy answered, *"not fair... you have to speak up.* That's what we doin."

"We don't have to leave!" the rapper shot back, "and we don't have rights when we let niggas like that fake one ovva there run over em."

"What the Hell? *What* did you call me, boy? I want them arrested," the judge insisted to the cop. "Now either you do it, or I'll call someone *else* out here to do it."

"They're just kids," the first cop protested, "and it *is* the *King* holiday comin up."

"Holiday, yunt! I've had about enough of you," growled Dolittle. "Your superiors will be hearing from me." He looked to the second cop, nodding. "And so will yours."

One minute later, all three teenagers were face-down on the sidewalk in handcuffs, where they stayed for 15 minutes before being shoved into a police car and taken away. Yet even as they lied there, they continued to sing and rap.

Then I go to my brother,
And I say, "brother, help me, please."
But he winds up... knocking me
Back down on my knees.

At length, the hour of shutting up the courthouse office arrived. With an ill-will, Dolittle rose from his desk and tacitly admitted that fact to the expectant clerk, who instantly shut off his computer and put on his hat.

"You'll want all day off Monday too, I suppose?" said Dolittle.

"If it's cool with you, sir, then it's cool with me."

"It's not cool, but whatever," the judge said. "It simply is not fair to me."

"Why not?" the clerk asked.

"To *pay* you for this holiday. You're not even one of them. Why would *you* celebrate it? It has nothing to do with you and your people, Heschel."

"That was the point he was trying to make," the clerk answered meekly. "I'm convinced we are all *one* people, all of us."

"I believe the same!" Dolittle insisted, "so why are we setting aside a day that will annually highlight our divisions?"

"You just don't get it, Thomas," Heschel said, but I'm equally convinced that with God all things are possible." And then he left.

Dolittle took his melancholy dinner in his usual melancholy restaurant, a rare winter special: a distinctive Georgia oyster stew. After having read all the newspapers, he spent the balance of his dinner hour reviewing upcoming cases, and then began walking home, which was a few blocks away.

As Dolittle strode along in the bitter cold, there came a-rushing toward him from the darkness a brown-skinned, voluptuous, troubled, and frightened blind woman. At once startled, he shoved her away, raising a clenched fist to threaten against further encroachment.

"What is your problem, woman!" Dolittle demanded. "You're disgusting! How dare you touch me!"

"I, I need your help," she wailed, falling to the ground, clinging to his leg. "Help me. You *know* me. I used to work for you. I'm begging you! Please help me!"

Dolittle carefully checked his surroundings as he "put hands on her" to shove her away again. He had heard stories of wily women approaching men, feigning distress, only to set them up for robbery or extortion.

"You stay away from me!" he insisted. "I don't know you! What do you want from me?"

"But you *do* know me!" she cried. "Don't you remember? I came out to find you because I thought you would help me. Out of decency!"

"I don't remember you, woman! What is your problem?" he asked.

"Please, Thomas! I'm in a bad place," she wept. "I'm being abused... by a group of powerful old men who you know! They've raped me, and they've forced me into a life of prostitution. They're pimping me out!"

On hearing those words, Dolittle abruptly turned away from her.

"Rape? Prostitution? I will not get involved in such a sordid matter," he said. "I refuse. You're making serious criminal accusations, Miss, where you obviously cannot and have not showed me any offer of proof. I suggest you take your complaint to the appropriate authorities and begin there."

"I've already gone to the appropriate damn authorities, Judge!" she protested. "They're part of the rapists! I came to you because you're my only hope. Your Honor—they've already destroyed my reputation and my esteem. Please don't let them take what's left of my soul!"

"I'll tell you what, woman," Dolittle sighed, handing her his card. "Come back to me when you have proof that you are being abused, raped and prostituted by this group of powerful men. Maybe then I'll be inclined to help you. For now, it's been a long day, and not to be rude—you're impeding my progress. Get away from me so I can go about my business!"

"I expected more from you," she sighed, resigning. "My name is Jussie T, so if you someday read about my untimely demise, only then you'll be sorry and ashamed you shunned me. *A man dies when he refuses to stand up for justice!*"

Dolittle lived in the condominium on G Street, which had once belonged to his deceased partner. It was a gloomy development that day, so the brown-painted bricks and white wood trim were set against the gray-black, ominous backdrop of a dark sky. He had thought to venture to move on many occasions, but deep within, he resented change. Innately, he feared progress. So, while he had explored other possibilities, he could not bring himself to change the status quo.

The building was old and dreary, and no one actually lived in it but Dolittle, as the other rooms were all being let out as offices. The yard outside was so dark that even Dolittle, who knew its every stone, stumbled and had to shine the flashlight from his phone along the ground to guide his steps as he made his way to the entrance.

Then fog, frost and snow obscured the features of the old black gate in front of the residence, and when Dolittle pulled it open, it protested the assault with a loud creaking groan that hung in the air and echoed through the stark, deserted neighborhood.

For all the time he was there, he always arrived to confront a large LED screen and keyboard to the left of the double doors. There had never been anything remarkable about it as he accessed it, whether morning, noon or night.

Notwithstanding, over decades, Dolittle had never once thought of his partner—not until before he was forced to mention Marshall, twenty-seven-years dead, that afternoon. However, as he stood before the door, there came the most unexplainable phenomenon. As Dolittle accessed the LED screen and panel, the normal menu did not appear. Instead, he saw Marshall's morbid ghostly face wavering in the high-resolution screen, staring back out at him.

Marshall's face. The features were distorted by a haze, but his semblance was unmistakable. It was eerily backlit, with a dismal heat to the light, so that Marshall had the appearance of an innocent man in a prison cell. His expression was not angry or ferocious, but he looked at Dolittle *as Marshall used to look at him*, though with his ghostly spectacles turned up upon its gossamer forehead.

The haint's hair, white and disheveled, glowed and yielded as if stirred by the breath of heat from a superheated furnace. The eyes were wide open, yet they were perfectly motionless. Unlike Dolittle remembered, the specter's ghastly and unnatural whiteness—with bright green bile trailing from the left corner of its lip, made the face appear horrible. But the expression on its face was not threatening. Rather, it seemed to bring Dolittle calm.

As he stared at the screen in disbelief, the shocking image dissolved to show the bright green LED security menu protocol again. For the first time, Dolittle experienced the sensation of his blood suddenly running cold. Awash with terror, he followed the protocol on the screen, dialed in his security code and opened the door.

"Virginia, lights on!" he yelled nervously before instant illumination.

After what he saw on the screen, he was not sure if he wanted to move about the condo. Next, he looked to the LED screen on the wall just inside the door, half-expecting Marshall's image to appear again, causing him to reflect on the Court. His colleagues joked that the Court was being haunted by "Marshall's Spark."

There was nothing on the wall next to the door, except the entry panel screen, and so he said, "This is total yunt!" and he closed the door with a bang. Inside, every sound, from the creaking of the floor under his muffled footsteps to the persistent ticking of the huge grandfather clock, reverberated through the space like a nightmare effect from a scene in a horror movie.

Every room above, and every step on every staircase in the hollow spaces below, seemed to have a separate peal of echoes of its own. Since Dolittle was not afraid of echoes, he sighed, locked the door, and went upstairs to his condo, checking his email messages and Twitter as he went.

Up Dolittle went, feeling more at home and at ease. He almost liked darkness, but only in secret at home. In the back of his mind, he sensed something supernatural, so he walked through the rooms of the great residence to see all was right before shutting his heavy door, Marshall's ghostly face still imprinted in his mind.

Quite satisfied after the initial search, he closed the door to his private dwelling and locked himself in—double-locked himself in, which was not his custom. Bathroom, bedroom, office and library inside—were all as they should be. Nothing under the table, nothing under the sofa. Thus secured against additional surprise, he took off his coat and tie, tossing them atop an ancient Parisian chaise lounge chair, put on his pajamas, robe, slippers and nightcap, and he sat down before the fire.

There were still heated, glowing coals in the small fireplace, so he put on one of the small logs, blowing to billow until it caught aflame. Craving his favorite late-night snack, he microwaved a small bowl of grits and added butter, salt and Louisiana hot sauce.

It was a stingy fire, providing little heat, veritably nothing on such a cold, bitter night. He scooted close to it, blowing at it again, trying to extract the least sensation of warmth from such a small log. The fireplace was an old one, built by some early American colonist long ago, and it was paved all round with quaint hand-made tiles, designed to illustrate the Scriptures.

There was Cain and Abel, Pharaoh's daughter, the Queen of Sheba, Angelic messengers descending through the air on clouds like featherbeds. There was Abraham, Belshazzar, Apostles putting off to sea in butter-boats, hundreds of figures to attract his thoughts. Yet that haunting face of Marshall, twenty-seven years dead, suddenly came onto the tiles, like the ancient Prophet's rod, to swallow up the whole.

If each of the smooth tiles had been blank screens at first, with the power to shape some picture on its surface from the disjointed fragments of Dolittle's thoughts, there then was a copy of old Marshall's face on every last one of them.

"I don't believe it!" Dolittle bellowed as he walked across the room.

After several turns, he sat down again, and his eyes fell upon a statue of Roman Janus, which his nephew had given him on King's birthday, one year earlier. After he threw his head back in the chair, his glance happened to rest upon the television, with a 75-inch high-definition screen, that hung in the room, although it was off.

Thus it was with great astonishment and with a strange and inexplicable dread, that as he looked, Dolittle saw the screen turn on, unprompted, displaying again the image of the ghostly Marshall. When he looked at his cell phone and his tablet, and both of those displayed the same image on their screens, and the same image was reflected on the large windows of the great room.

This might have lasted half a minute, or a minute, but it seemed an hour. The images disappeared as they had begun, together. They were succeeded by a clanking noise, deep down below, in the building's cellar—as if some tortured, enslaved person was dragging a heavy chain up the staircases in the building. Dolittle then remembered to have heard that ghosts in haunted houses were described as "dragging chains."

He felt a sense of foreboding after a chill ran over his skin, raising hairs and instant goosebumps that leapt up on his arms and legs. He felt a cold sweat on his forehead. A mirror on the wall to his left beckoned a glance, and when he looked over, he saw his *own* reflection and recoiled as he watched his hair, flesh, face and lower jaw dissolve, leaving there a chapfallen skull, gibe-less and witless as Yorick.

Hardly believing his eyes, he neared the mirror, terrified that the appearance of the skull portended his demise, or worse—his own death. Then, when staring closely at the face of the skull, Dolittle watched as twin luminescent brown cankerworms appeared at each of the eye sockets, the loops in their bodies giving the skull the appearance of having glowing eyes, filled with dour judgment.

Even before he could respond, the cankerworms quickly transformed into shining moths, flying up toward the noontime nighttime sky. After watching them disappear, his normal face and appearance returned.

Immediately, he heard the cellar-door fly open with a booming sound, a loud bang, and then he heard a noise much louder, a heavy chain dragging along the floors below, coming up the stairs, toward his room, and then coming straight towards his door.

"This is yunt still!" said Dolittle. "I don't believe it."

His color darkened though, when without a pause, it came on through the heavy door and passed into the room before his eyes. When the spirit arrived, the dying flame leaped up, as though it cried, "I know him! It's Marshall's Ghost!" and fell again.

It was the same face, the very same—Marshall in his spectacles, his usual suit, briefcase and the curly gray hair upon his head. The rusted chain he drew was wrapped around his waist. It was long and wound about him, like a tail, and it was weighted. In terror, Dolittle estimated its weight—the accumulated burden of court cases, trials, arguments, opinions, appeals, and politics, wrought in iron. The specter's body was transparent so that Dolittle, observing him and looking through his waistcoat, could see the wallet in his back pocket.

Dolittle had often heard it said that Marshall's transparency would be his undoing, but he had never believed it until then.

No, nor did he believe it even then. Though he looked the phantom through and through, he saw it standing before him. He felt the chilling influence of its death-cold eyes, and he could see the folds and stitching in the fabric of the oversized bandana that was wrapped around over his head and under his chin. Dolittle gawked because he hadn't noticed it at first. He blinked hard and wagged his head, still not trusting his eyes. He hoped he was somehow asleep.

"What's going on, Thoroughgood? Am I lucid dreaming? Are you in my mind?" Dolittle asked, caustic, cold and angry as ever. "What do you want from me?"

"Much!"

It was Marshall's voice, no doubt about it.

"Who are you?" Dolittle asked.

"Ask me who I *was*."

"Who *were* you then?" Dolittle groaned, raising his voice. "You're familiar, for a haint."

He was going to say, "for a nigga," but he substituted the former as more appropriate.

"My name is *Conscientia*. In life I was your partner, Thoroughgood Marshall."

"Hold on, whoever you are, or were. Are you, are you able to sit down?" asked Dolittle, looking doubtfully at the visitor.

"I can."

"Do it, then."

Dolittle asked the question because he didn't know whether a haint so transparent might find himself in a condition to take a chair. He didn't want to embarrass the haint by asking it to do something impracticable. Yet the haint sat down on the opposite side of the fireplace, as if he were quite used to it.

"You don't believe in me, do you?" observed the haint.

"I don't," Dolittle answered, wagging his head.

"What evidence *would* you believe that I stand before you as Marshall… beyond that of your senses?"

"I don't know," said Dolittle. "I see you… and I smell you. Woo!"

"Why do you doubt your senses?"

"Because," Dolittle answered, "little things can cause them to defy reality. Something as simple as an upset stomach could have created you. You might be an undigested cobb salad from lunch, maybe a little too much Louisiana hot sauce on my grits, or the cheese on them that was beyond its sell-by date. How do I know if you aren't that odd mushroom from dinner tonight? Or you could be the nagging gas in my gut, begging to be passed in one way or another."

Dolittle wasn't much in the habit of joking, which is why he felt strange about going there. Unnerved at the horrific sight before his eyes, he did it to distract his *own* attention, and his impulse to flee the room, condo and building. The creepy voice of Marshall's haint disturbed him to the very marrow of his bones.

Sitting and feeling forced to stare into those fixed, glazed eyes in silence made Dolittle want to panic. There was something else, something awful, that betrayed his senses: it seemed that even though it was sitting right in front of him, the haint seemed to *exist* in a separate dimension—obviously a greatly heated place, as Dolittle could hear a crackling fire and feel the radiated heat. Droplets of sweat on his forehead tickled as they merged and began to drip down his face.

Manifesting from this infernal dimension, the specter of Marshall sat perfectly motionless, while shadows of flames lit and darkened its agonized face. All the while, its hair and shirt were stirred, animated by drafts from unseen flames. Yet worse, the spirit's piercing unblinking eyes never strayed from those of Dolittle.

"I ate a peculiar-tasting wild mushroom tonight," Dolittle said, remembering his dinner of Georgia oyster stew, when a strange morsel had caused him to pause. In mentioning it, he had hoped, if even for a second, to divert the vision's stony gaze away from himself.

"I saw that," replied the haint.

"How? You weren't there," Dolittle complained.

"But I saw it all the same," the haint insisted, "notwithstanding."

"Well!" Dolittle sighed, "perhaps when I swallowed it, it caused a mild symptom of hallucination that summoned you, and yet by eating another, I could summon a legion of fantasy creatures, far worse than you."

"I *was* that mushroom," the haint replied, "irritating your soul, providing for you a pearl and a vision, if you would only see its value.

Dolittle tapped his left temple. "I don't know how, but you exist in my head. Somehow, I *created* you up here, and I can send you back whatever infernal realm you came from. You're not real, I tell you! You don't scare me!"

In response, the spirit bellowed in a horrible, dark threatening roar that shattered the chandelier, which came crashing down toward Dolittle, who quickly dodged aside to narrowly escape being crushed. Then the haint shook its heavy chain so violently that the huge iron links obliterated Dolittle's desk and computer. Fallen back into his office chair, Dolittle held on tight to keep himself from completely losing his bowels.

He thought nothing could be more frightening, but then the haint, it then began to unwind the extra-long bandana, unwrapping from the top of its head and around the chin, again and again, until... Dolittle was unprepared when he saw it, when he heard the thud, but when the final layer yielded, the haint's lower jaw, unconnected by flesh or ligaments, fell, dropping into the phantom's waiting hand near what would be its waist.

Horrified, Dolittle fell to his knees, clasping his hands before his face.

"Good lawd, man!" he exclaimed. "What the hell are you? And what do you want from me?"

"Man of temporal worldly mind!" replied the haint. "I ask again, do you believe in me, or not?"

"I see you," said Dolittle. "In this strange case, I sense I must believe what I see and what you are! But why would spirits walk the earth, and why would one come to me?"

"It is required of every man," the haint returned, "that the spirit within him must bear the weight of his legacy, and men given great power and responsibility must fulfill a destiny greater than themselves. But if that man does not do it in life, then his spirit is condemned to do it after death—doomed to wander through a world of wasted opportunity and enlightenment. Oh, woe is me! To witness what I cannot fulfill—but might have fulfilled on Earth... and my legacy turned to a greater good and a better outcome!"

Again, the haint raised a cry and shook its chain while wringing its shadowy hands.

"But why are you are chained? And locked-up?" asked Dolittle, trembling. "You of all people? Tell me why."

"I wear the chain I forged in life and exist in the prison I built," replied the haint. "Both, I fashioned for myself in my wasted life. Despite the fights I waged, I created my tortures, link by link, brick by brick and yard by yard. I am chained because I was not warned, and because I was not warned, I am in this hellish prison cell where I am incarcerated. If you still don't believe, think again. Take a moment to consider the chain and prison cell that *you* have forged."

Dolittle trembled more and more.

"Can you imagine," the haint continued, "the sheer weight and length of the chain that *you* have fashioned for yourself? Your chain was already longer and thicker than mine thirty years ago when you were confirmed. Since then, you've molded for yourself a ponderous, monstrous chain! It will be your tormenter, your prison, for all time."

Dolittle glanced behind himself to the floor, expecting to discover a rusted coiled chain, the size of a mountain, but he saw nothing.

"Thoroughgood," Dolittle pleaded thoroughly concerned. "Old Thoroughgood Marshall—tell me more! But tell me something good, Thoroughgood."

"I have none to tell you," the haint replied. "That will come from other voices in your life, Thomas Dolittle, when you've learned who they are and what they are telling you. All I can be is real with you tonight. Not much more I can do for you. To my regret, I never considered my legacy beyond the narrow walls of our courthouse. In life, my spirit ventured little beyond the narrow limits of my judicial role, so now I'm forced to realize the outcome: I am a judge, now sitting in judgment!"

It was a habit with Dolittle. Whenever he became thoughtful, he put his hands in his pockets. Pondering on what the haint had said, he did so then, though without lifting his eyes or getting off his knees.

"You must have been very slow about learning that lesson, Thoroughgood," Dolittle observed in a business-like manner, though with humility and deference.

"Slow?" the haint repeated.

"You have been twenty-seven years dead," mused Dolittle. "And you've been *realizing* it all that time?"

"The whole time," said the haint. "No rest, no peace. It's been an incessant torture of remorse."

"Come on, man," Dolittle urged. "That's a lot of realizing in twenty-seven years. What is so hard to understand?"

The haint, on hearing this, set up another cry and clanked its chain so hideously in the dead silence of the night that the D.C. government attorney would have been justified in indicting it for a nuisance.

"Still you cannot see! I am incarcerated! Bound, double-ironed and locked-up!" cried the haint. "Imagine what torture of incarceration is for immortal creatures! The only real Justice is God. There is but one earthly judge who was, or who *is* good, while the well-intended on Earth only *believe* in the goodness of their judgment. They can strive to follow footsteps, but all fall short.

"All attempted justice is but little to the greater justice, and to think otherwise is arrogance. Thus in my arrogance, I fell short! Oh, poor Thomas, I fell short of our legacy!"

"But you were always a good and honest judge, Thoroughgood," faltered Dolittle, who now began to apply this standard to himself.

"History is the place where judges are judged. I should have done more!" the haint grieved, I could have done so much more for justice. I think of all the times I compromised, the times when I was swayed, was pressured. I am haunted by the memories of those times when I did not hold to the righteous convictions in my heart!

"No, Thoroughgood, this has not *happened* to you!" Dolittle insisted.

"Behind me, human concerns! O Justice!" cried the haint, wringing its ephemeral hands again. "It was bigger than me, more than my subjective opinions and causes. Justice was my duty! Our people and the common welfare were my business. Equity for the loss of black lives was my duty. Equality, opportunity, mercy, forbearance and leveling the field were all my business. Yet despite all that I did, my personal accomplishments—they were nothing but a drop within a vast sea, which is the comprehensive cause of Justice—past, present and yet-to-come!"

The haint held up its chain at arm's length, as if that link was the cause of all its unavailing grief, and he dropped it heavily on the ground again.

"At this time of the year, as we all reflect," it said, "I suffer most. I rue that I did not consider what would come, and why I did not, in my place, more carefully consider holding police and private citizens more accountable for the killing of unarmed black and brown people, the consequences of mass incarceration resulting from disparity and inequality in sentencing. I saw the future with a moderate eye, though never with the other, more progressive eye.

"The tiny seed becomes the tree and then the tree bears fruit. The ponderance of history weighs mightily on me, and heavier in course of time. If only I had known, I could have chosen better seed and watered more, more carefully considered who and what was vulnerable. I could have done a greater good for Justice! The opportunity was wasted, lost in me, in my portion of our legacy!"

Dolittle was very much dismayed to hear the haint going on at this rate so that he began to tremble.

"*Hear me*, man!" cried the haint. "My time is nearly gone."

"I am hearing you!" sweating, shivering Dolittle then said, "and I worry for my own soul. Don't sugarcoat it! I want the truth, if even in your tortured testimony, Thoroughgood! Be real. I need to know the truth!"

"I do not yet know *how* I'm here before you in a shape that you can see," the haint said, "when you never could see me before. I've sat invisible beside you for many days."

"Aw! Seriously? That's awkward…" Dolittle shivered and wiped more perspiration from his dark brow. It was not an agreeable idea.

"That is the most important part of my punishment," continued the haint. "I am here tonight to warn you that you might have a narrow chance and hope of escaping my fate. I can save you from my torments, Thomas! I want to."

"I never realized it, but your example was always a good aspiration for me," said Dolittle. "All good. Please, help me!"

"You will be haunted," resumed the ancient Thoroughgood, "by Three Haints."

Dolittle's countenance fell almost as low as his associate's jaw had.

"Is that the 'chance and hope' you mentioned, Thoroughgood?" Dolittle asked in a faltering voice.

"It is."

"I—eh, three *more* haints, like you? I don't think so," said Dolittle. "I'm not really feeling that's necessary."

"Without their visits," said the haint, "you'll be much worse off than me. Just expect the first tomorrow at one o'clock a.m."

"Couldn't I hear em all at once and get this matter over with?" asked Dolittle.

"Expect the second on the next night at the same hour. The third upon the next night when your Virginia app announces it is one o'clock. You don't have to worry about seeing me again. I've done my job—I've warned you. And if you know what's good for you, you will not disregard my warning. Mind your legacy!"

When it had said these words, the haint took the bandana from the table, and after raising its slack jaw with its left hand, it wrapped the fabric firmly around its head. Dolittle heard and felt the sensation of teeth grinding as the knot tightened, binding the jaw. When he raised his eyes again, the hideous haint was in his face, frightfully close, with its chain wrapped around its arm.

It walked backward from him, and with each step back, the window raised itself a little until it was wide open.

The haint beckoned Dolittle to approach, which he did. When they were close, Marshall's Haint held up its hand, warning him to come no nearer. Dolittle stopped.

Standing there, Dolittle felt a chill on his skin, followed by another sudden rash of tingling skin. Straining, he could hear seeming distant eerie noises in the air, the wails of suffering souls and the incoherent sounds of sadness and rue, of weeping and wanting, of wretched realization of regret.

The ghostly specter, after listening for a moment, joined the dissonant chorus of humming blues before levitating and drifting out on the ethereal billows of a breeze in the stark dark night.

Dolittle went to the windowsill, his curiosity outpacing his fear.

As he looked out, the air was filled with gossamer shapes and backlit shadows, gliding on air currents here and there, all desperate to reach a destination, without knowing what the end would be. They all wore chains, like Marshall's Haint. The ones that Dolittle recognized were former congress members and some were judicial and justice department appointees, but the greater part were cabinet officials, presidential appointees and media personalities.

Many were linked together, though none were free. He definitely recognized one chained old ghost in a black robe, known for a commerce clause, who cried piteously at being unable to represent a wretched old man with a penchant for lying, whom it saw below, standing before a helicopter. The misery lied in the fact that these spirits, upon repentance, earnestly sought to interfere for good in human affairs, but because they were dead, they had lost the power they squandered forever, *no longer any share in what is done under the sun.*

Whether these repentant souls dissolved into the mist or a suffocating fog concealed them, he could not tell. Yet their wails and regrets seemed to be drawn into the distant darkness, and the night became as still as it had been when Dolittle had walked home.

He closed the window and examined the door through which the haint had entered. It remained double-locked— bottom lock and dead-bolt, a door he had locked with his own hands, and the locks were undisturbed. He tried to say "Yunt..." but he stopped halfway through the word.

It could have been the shock, the growing sense of PTSD he felt, or it could have been the impossible encounter with a supernatural phenomenon and the dreadful conversation with a haint, but he was exhausted to the point of delusion, his senses overwhelmed, drained. Stumbling, he went straight to bed without setting an alarm or engaging in his regular bathroom routine. He fell asleep within seconds, and he slept as if he had overindulged in his reliable old French brandy.

SHOUT II

SHOUT II
The First of The Three Haints

When Dolittle awoke, it was so dark that, squinting from the bed to the LED display on the nightstand, he could scarcely distinguish the mist-covered window from the frosted walls of his bedroom. He stared, trying to pierce the darkness with furrowed eyes, when the alarm on his cell phone startled him, causing him to sit erect.

To his great astonishment, from his nightstand, the Virginia personal assistant device's alarm feature's voice began to announce the time, though at an accelerated pace.

"It's six o'clock a.m., Thomas. It's seven o'clock a.m. It's eight o'clock a.m.… It's two o'clock p.m.… It's six o'clock p.m.…" Thus in rapid succession, day came and moved toward night until… "It's twelve o'clock a.m."

It made no sense. When he went to bed, it was just minutes past two a.m. The digital clock had to be wrong! An Internet virus had somehow infected the Smarthome app! Midnight? Was it the next night?

"Virginia!" he called out, "What time is it? What time is it in Washington D.C. right now?"

"It's 12:01 a.m. Sleep well, Thomas," the voice from the speaker returned.

"No. That's impossible!" groaned Dolittle. "There's no way I could have slept through the night and then through the entire next day so that it's midnight again…two hours *before* I went to bed last night! He looked to the window, squinting toward a dark sky, with clouds and a few stars. "Virginia's wrong! It must be *noon*. Had she said "p.m.?" *Could it be an eclipse of the sun or some other heavenly omen?*

Suddenly agitated, he hurried up from the bed and clambered toward the window, which was frosted over.

From deep within, he summoned the heat of his core to his breath as he blew, turning white ice crystals dark before using the sleeve of his pajamas to wipe away an opening so he could peek outside. The landscape was still and frozen, almost surreal. Streets that would be busy at noon were empty and silent, without even a breeze daring to challenge the cold. If the sun was there, it yielded to the moment.

Somewhat relieved and convinced that he was either dreaming or confused, Dolittle went to bed again. He thought and thought, thinking to make sense of it over and over, but he could make nothing of it. The more he thought, the deeper down the hole he descended, and the more he tried not to think, the more he thought.

The appearance of Marshall's Haint and its warning had done a number on Dolittle's brain. Every time he managed his thoughts enough to logically conclude that Marshall and the visitation was no more than a dream, it seemed he heard the voice again, and he experienced flashbacks even more real and terrible than the actual visit. His bedroom still seemed to be quaking. *Was it a dream, or not?*

So Dolittle lay there, agitated and unsettled, until he looked over at the digital clock that showed 12:45, and only then did he remember Marshall warned him that the First Haint would come at 1:00 a.m. Dolittle figured he'd stay awake until the hour was passed, and since there was no way he could sleep with so much stirring in his head, he poured a brandy and waited.

That fifteen minutes took so long that Dolittle was convinced that time, like everything outside his window, had frozen still. He wondered if he had fallen asleep or transitioned into dreaming with his eyes still open. The black and Latino ne'er-do-wells who had come into his office earlier—the same ones asking for the donation—had they conceived some devious way to drug him? Real did not seem real, and what he saw, he did not, could not believe. Was he awake, or was he dreaming he was awake?

The First of the Three Haints 39

When the digital clock showed 1 a.m., still nothing happened. "Ah!" Dolittle sighed. "I was just dreaming," he laughed. Three haints indeed! Thirty seconds later, virtual assistant Virginia's voice broke the silence, unprompted.

"The time is 1:00 a.m. Stay awake, Thomas. You have a visitor."

"Uh... no," said Dolittle, looking over at the speaker that mocked his peace. "No visitors, Virginia. I'm going to sleep so I can wake," he insisted as he retreated under traditionalist covers.

In that moment, the blanket and sheets of his bed were snatched off by an invisible hand and thrown to the floor. His skin tingled and became instantly prickly and sensitive to the slightest movement in the air. He felt it—something was coming right at him. He sat up rigidly in fright and tightly shut his eyes, though he knew time and curiosity would pry them open again.

He definitely felt a *presence* in the room, and someone or something had snatched off his bedding, but when he looked out, he was alone, though he heard something on the other side of the door.

It was the sudden sounds of drums, the *dejembes*, speaking in an African tongue, accompanied by the *dununs*, with *shekere* and *kese kese* accents. Then he heard the sound of rhythmic stomping outside before a force collided with the door, obliterating it, turning it into a smoking, smoldering scattering of wood chips.

Next, the source of that force appeared in the doorway. It was the biggest, blackest man Dolittle had ever seen in his life. Purple blue-black, the incredibly muscular buck, in the tattered threadbare clothing of a slave, stood over nine-feet tall as he continued to dance, jumping and leaping, shaking the foundation of the house with every time he landed on the wooden floor.

This big bald nigga done broke down my door! Dolittle thought.

Fearing for his life, he decided to "stand his ground," and so reaching into his bureau, Dolittle retrieved his loaded Glock-9 and raised it, aimed, and shot the invader at center mass. Just to make sure, he emptied the entire clip.

Instead of falling to the ground, the huge black man only laughed. "*Kutupa kokoto hakuwezi kuniumiza*," he laughed with blue-black gums as he hocked up one of the shells, cracked it in his gleaming white teeth, and spat it to the ground, like an empty sunflower seed.

"Thomas Dolittle," the giant slave said in broken English, swatting the gun to the floor "Do John Henry scare you? *Burnt-up black boy!* Why is black so *scary* to you, my son?"

"I shot you!" Dolittle muttered in disbelief. "You're not real. You did not die. I *must* be dreaming!"

"Your life, Thomas, is a broken-wing bird that cannot *fly*," it answered, cracking and spitting another silvery shell casing.

"Are you the First Haint who Marshall said would come?"

"Not I," the creature answered, "I am but the *presage* to the First Haint, who is already *here*."

Saying that, the huge black buck transformed into a wispy black smoke that filled the room, becoming darkness itself.

Now frightened, Dolittle cringed as he took small steps forward, until he found a wall, and fumbling along the wall, he stumbled into a table, and a lamp. Trembling fingers discovered the turn switch. With a click, the dim light came on.

When his eyes regained focus, he found himself face-to-face with the hideous unearthly specter who had snatched his blanket and sheet, and he was staring directly into the ghoulish, decomposing sneering countenance of an angry, radical old man. As he looked into its eyes, he felt an unrelenting force drawing him closer. He feared falling into that reaching, undeserving, vengeful tortured soul.

Pale and frightening, the creature's huge, oversized face had the appearance of an old white chap, while it had the aspect and mannerisms of someone familiar to him—his grandfather, an old black man. Its face lacked color. However, its eyes, deep chasms, were the blackest black, and when he looked into them, he felt a great quivering at the pit of his soul, to the core of his being. His bowels spasmed, dropped and seemed to become liquid mush, drawn toward the great gravity from the presence... until he forced himself to look away.

Dolittle glanced side-eye, noting the straight white hair on the head of the huge face was thinning, and the thick beard and mustache were similarly lacking pigment. Yet there was something in the composition of its facial features—the nose, lips and the area around the eyes—he could see it. He innately knew, though the buckra never saw it, no matter how obvious.

From his early years, Dolittle along with his tiny neighborhood and communities across the American South, always knew immediately who "was" and who "wasn't". Sometimes the old folks and the griots would whisper the rumors, supported by secret alternative genealogies. This First Haint *was*, but who?

It wore a black formal jacket and vest, with a white shirt and silk ribbon bowtie. Its neck and body seemed too small for the huge decaying head, though the body did not seem to struggle under the stunning disproportion. It held in its small hands a hammer, and awl and an ax, which was a source of unease for Dolittle. Were they tools, or were they weapons of torture? And yet, tucked under its arm was an ancient original paper scroll with Calson font lettering, though not quite new. A little worn.

As he finally peered directly upon the First Haint's face, Dolittle realized that, though its head was perhaps four or five times bigger than his own, its actual face was no bigger than his was. Despite the enigmatic time distortion, where a second seemed like an hour, the back of its head, bluish veins pulsating, seemed to be burgeoning, growing before his eyes. Dolittle wondered as he watched if the head would explode or continue to grow to monstrous proportions and fill the room. The creature was difficult to behold. What was in that gigantic head? Was it developing brain matter, or merely heated air?

"Are *you* the First Haint who Marshall said would haunt me?" Dolittle quivered as he asked.

"*Mais oui, je suis le meme*," it answered, "I certainly am not the last, while I am second to none. *Je m'appelle Pathos*. In English, I am called Pathos."

Oh, its foul, fetid breath! Its first voice was soft, but a second voice resonated in a sort of haunting echo, sounded in a distinctly darker, deeper, ominous tone.

"Who are you?" Dolittle demanded. "And exactly *what* are you?"

"*Je suis le Haint de injustice passé*," it said. "I am the Haint of Injustice Past."

"Past?" Dolittle inquired.

Though the ghost's bubbling, melting face was dreadful, Dolittle could not resist his innate urge to argue. "Then that would make you irrelevant," he said. "What's passed is past. Even God has no power to change the past."

"More specifically, the future's past," it said, "the past of Present and Future Injustice. The past I represent is relevant to both because it can change the present and future of injustice."

"Which is my very proof that the past should *remain* in the past," Dolittle debated, "since *ipso facto*, it cannot be changed."

"But never forgotten, lest all three do frightful harm."

Frightful, Dolittle thought. *That big head of yours sho is enough to scare me!* "Do you mind if I pour myself a brandy?" he asked. "I really need one now! I'll pour you one

The First of the Three Haints

too. You look like you could use one. Do spirits... you know, *do* spirits?"

He hadn't meant to ask as a joke. It just came out that way. In response, the First Haint scowled.

"*T'es con ou quoi?* I am here on grave business, Thomas," the deep bass echo resonating, threatening. "What? Would you seek to dull my sense of purpose, or yours in such a sacred responsibility?"

"I'll take that as a no. I'm having one though," Dolittle said as he rose and poured a brandy from the crystal decanter into a snifter. Yet no sooner did he pour it, the snifter became consumed in flames so hot that Dolittle dropped it to the ground, where it shattered violently.

Fire spilled out across the floor and continued to burn brightly without seeming to consume the wood under it. Moreover, the decanter, sitting on the carved wooden bar cabinet, was also obscured in flames.

"I'm sorry!" Dolittle cried out, staring at his scorched fingertips, which were burned and throbbed in pain. "That feels real!"

"Look around, Thomas," the First Haint said. "Consequences are always real. You merely have not allowed them to exist in your mind, not until tonight, not until by compulsion."

Dolittle reached out and grabbed the decanter with his other hand, but he quickly drew it back, singed and smoking, his palm charred and blistering.

"Dammit!" he screamed, gripping his wrist. "What is this? What is the point? What is your purpose?"

"Your welfare," replied the First Haint.

"My welfare? I was sleeping just fine until you came in and ripped off my blanket."

He looked over to see the sheets were aflame. The fire had crawled across the room to climb the window drapes, as well as the walls and door, which were consumed in hot evaporation.

"I came to save you, *ton pauvre âme*," the First Haint said. "You can't stay here." Head wobbling slightly, it extended a firm hand while turning toward the window. "Come with me. We need to go out there into the world."

"You started this fire! Out where?" Dolittle demanded. "We're three stories up with no ladder. I weigh 230 and haven't been to the gym in months. That's a no!"

As he looked back at the room and the blazing, crackling fire, he realized the roaring hissing flames had begun devouring all they touched. Wearing only his pajamas and robe, he felt the incredible temperature to the core of his being, an infernal heat, hotter than fire. Only then did he—dream, or no dream—begin to fear for his very life. He looked out the window down toward the ground and cringed, clinging to the First Haint's cold hard arm, pleading.

"I… I can't climb down there," Dolittle stammered. "I'll fall and I'll be crippled, or I'll die! Maybe you can fly or whatever, but I can't, and I'm not about to risk it."

"Be cool," the First Haint said. "There is so much you've yet to understand. Hold onto me with one hand, and when I float out there, you'll float out there with me. Just don't look down if you're afraid of heights."

Dolittle clutched the First Haint's arm with both hands, and in that moment, they passed through the wall. As Dolittle looked around, he realized they had re-materialized in a courtroom, though one unlike the courtroom he knew. There definitely was something "familiar" about the spirit that resided there. The arch, the columns and even the lighting fixtures—it was definitely not his courtroom, though similar.

The nine illuminated seats at the front of the room were occupied by nine worn old men, dressed in worn old-white skin, worn old-white hair and worn old-white attitudes, nine old-white men who looked alike, spoke alike and thought alike, though one was slightly different. One of the nonuplets he immediately recognized! The man's judicial voice, tenor and spirit were unmistakable, as he was none other than Melville Weston Fuller, Chief Justice from 1888 to 1910.

"And I know who that other one is!" Dolittle said. "That's Justice Steven Field… and there's, there's Justice John Harland. It's obvious we've somehow been transported to an alternate time and place?"

"Arguments in Plessy versus Ferguson on April 13, 1896," the First Haint replied.

"That was a 7-1 decision," Dolittle interrupted, speaking as if by rote. "The Court found that racial segregation in Louisiana and the rest of the South *didn't* violate the Fourteenth Amendment's Equal Protection Clause, violating rights of Negros, who became your present-day African Americans."

"It was the worst ruling in the history of the U.S. Supreme Court," the First Haint insisted.

"You obviously have a bias," Dolittle countered, motioning to a seeming white man at a table, "since isn't that who you *were*, Pathos, when you were alive, sitting next to Counsel Tourgée there? Yes…wasn't Albion Tourgée Plessy's attorney?"

"*Bien sûr, Monsieur*, you are correct," the First Haint slowly nodded. So… you know something of this case?"

"Know it?" Dolittle scoffed. "Why I could brief it in my sleep! If you were Homer Plessy, you had no real interest in the matter. You made shoes for a living. You were recruited for it by activists and outside agitators."

"By *le Comité des Citoyens*, in 1892," the First Haint confirmed. "*Oui.*"

"You mean by the Citizen's Committee," Dolittle said, "the creoles of New Orleans, black and white. In 1890, Louisiana passed the Separate Car Act, a law requiring separate accommodations by race—basically 'segregation' in principle. The railroad was against the law because it meant they had to buy more cars, but the Committee wanted to repeal the act."

As their eyes focused on Plessy in the courtroom, Dolittle glanced back over at the First Haint, trying to discern a similarity. Slowly, he saw it—in the decaying creature and memory that Plessy had become.

"The Committee picked you only because you looked white. You were mixed, so you could 'pass' as white, but by their standard then, you were considered a Negro. So they got you to buy a ticket on the 'white only' car and had their own detective arrest you to test the law."

"*Bien sûr*," the First Haint said, "since in the 'past-perfect,' smaller plan for things, they knew they stood little chance of winning. Yet in the larger scheme, the case would demonstrate the unvarnished and undeniable injustice of the past, which would lend perspective to the present and the future."

"I don't know that," Dolittle said, "but Louisiana criminal district court judge John Ferguson ruled that racial segregation did *not* violate constitutional rights of the Negros. The decision was appealed then to that U.S. Supreme Court, where it was heard and upheld in 1896, and thus racial segregation became the legal law of the land."

"Indeed, Thomas," the First Haint agreed, "in schools, facilities, in jobs, transportation and housing."

"It was a 7-to-1 ruling and one I agree with in principle," Dolittle said. "Segregation laws should appropriately fall within the police power of the individual *states*. I support the Court's rationale then, that if a state legislature believed in good faith that its laws requiring segregation were reasonable and not designed to oppress a particular class, then those laws were legal."

"And the alternative argument?" the First Haint asked. "Have you also considered that?"

"Alternative argument? The decision was 7-to-1, with only Justice Harlan dissenting—nearly unanimous," Dolittle sighed, incredulous. "Did a sole dissenting opinion matter then, and much less now?"

"It matters in the present, and the future," the First Haint answered. "*Ergo*, the real question: what then is the legacy of injustice past?"

"Impossible to know," Dolittle answered quickly without deliberation.

"Then let me open the eyes of your soul to your past, Thomas. Behold!"

As the words were spoken, Dolittle and the First Haint passed through another wall and stood on the campus of a Roman Catholic boarding school near Savannah, Georgia, upon an open country road, with fields on either hand. Dolittle's erstwhile city had entirely vanished. Not a vestige of it was to be seen. The darkness and the mist had vanished with it, for it was a clear, cold, wintry day, with snow upon the ground.

"Good Lord!" said Dolittle, clasping his hands together as he looked around. "Saint Benedict, the Moor— my Catholic seminary school! My *segregated* Catholic seminary school. I have memories here!"

"Yes! Memories of a past," the First Haint reminded him.

"You're right. It was a time of profound turmoil for me— the first time I remember facing discrimination based on the color of my skin—and that discrimination came from black people, no less."

"Black people?" the First Haint asked.

"You wouldn't understand," Dolittle sighed. "It was coming from privileged, damn-near-white blacks like you, who created a blasted caste system, where the darker-skinned blacks were ranked the worst, judged as unintelligent and sub-human. It came from 'blacks' like *you*. They taunted me, ridiculing me as 'ABC—America's Blackest Child.'"

"And that informed your early opinions?" the First Haint asked.

"Not really, but I became attuned to detest all forms of discrimination, regardless of source or context," Dolittle answered. "I've experienced discrimination from both blacks and whites. Believe me, one is no less reprehensible than the other."

"Is that the most profound memory from your youth?"

"No," said Dolittle, as if surprised by a suddenly returned recollection.

In that instant, they stood in a segregated classroom where a much younger Dolittle had a seat at the back of a room full of white students, irrelevant and invisible.

"That's me at Conception Seminary College in Missouri!" Dolittle exclaimed. "I remember that day, that moment..."

"So far in the past?" the First Haint asked.

"It was Thursday, April 4, 1968," Dolittle recalled. "I remember it because Dr. Martin Luther King, Jr. was shot on a Memphis balcony that afternoon—a priest had just announced the assassination. I was a student of King, so I felt all hope betrayed, completely disillusioned. I was overwhelmed by a profound feeling of desperation and despair, and then that idiot said it."

"Who? He said what?"

"That fellow liberal, that compassionate Christian—I thought until then. I don't remember his name," Dolittle sneered, still disgusted. "I suppose it doesn't matter now, but he revealed the hypocrisy of the white liberal heart..."

Both looked on as a male white student, favored by the priesthood, exalted by the faculty, privileged by American society, responded to the announcement.

"Shot? Good! I hope that SOB died!" the model seminary student at the front of the class exclaimed, intentionally glancing back over his shoulder to train his eyes on Dolittle.

"That was the moment for me," the pajamaed, Dolittle, emotion returning, said to the First Haint, "when the disingenuousness of liberal whites became explicitly manifest. It was the first time I understood the obligation and purpose of my own radicalization. If I didn't spend my life challenging that false portrayal—that insincerity, that duplicity from whites, who were the supposed patrons and partners in the black struggle for justice, then I would never be true to the values superimposed on my soul by my stern grandfather."

"He never understood?" the First Haint asked.

"When I told him that I could no longer tolerate white duplicity and institutional and systemic racism, he reminded me that *his* standards, by contrast, were unalterable, regardless of my epiphany. Non-compliance meant separation. He was highly displeased with me."

The First Haint gazed upon Dolittle sadly. Its gentle touch, though it had been light and instantaneous, appeared still present to the judge's sense of feeling. He was conscious of a thousand memories floating in the air, each one connected with a thousand thoughts, hopes and joys, and cares long, long, forgotten.

"Your lip is trembling," said the First Haint. "Your semblance is quaking, and what is that upon your cheek?"

Dolittle seemed to revert to the nostalgic Gullah tongue, muttering a few unintelligible words—with an unusual accent in his voice. "Nothing. It's just a birthmark," he said, smearing his cheek, and he begged the First Haint to lead him where it would.

"Do you remember the way to your grandfather's house?" inquired the First Haint.

"Remember it?" sighed Dolittle, shaking his head "Why I could walk there with a blindfold on!"

"Strange that you have forgotten all the lessons from that time and place," the First Haint observed, "yet you force me to trust the power of your memory? Take me there."

As they walked along the road, Dolittle recognized every gate, post and tree until a little community appeared in the distance, with its bridge, its church, and a slowly winding river. Mr. Joe Wilson's son walked a mule along a fringe dirt trail, while a shiny new Chevy Bel Air containing two white teenaged couples sped by on a paved road on the far right.

Dolittle and the First Haint came upon the entrance to the colored neighborhood, where people bustled by, engaged in the daily activities of men buying goods from the general store, women in uniforms headed to domestic jobs in white folks homes, boys and girls with books, walking toward the school, laborers standing in truck beds, headed to the fields, all fully engaged in life, oblivious to the implication of their place in history.

Despite the injustice and its associate poverty, they were in great spirits and seemed to relish, with even a degree of percipience, their roles upon the stage.

"These are but shadows of the things that have been," said the First Haint. "They can't see us, and certainly are unable to fathom you could ever exist."

Yet and still, the community hustled about, passing by Dolittle and the First Haint, yes, and some kids, playing a game of chase, even passed *through* them. Dolittle knew and named every one of them.

"That's Bae-bae—ol Mista Taylor's daughter. Now she know she ain't supposeta be chasin after boys. And that fella in the corna over there sneakin a cigarette—that's my younger brother. I need ta go over and pop him upside his head!"

He was beyond all joy to return to his old neighborhood and his past, strangely so dear in his recollection. It was an interdependent community where people, despite their differences, knew and cared about each other. They realized that what affected the least among them affected all. The most ambitious boy there innately knew that even if he succeeded, they were bound by that shared experience of determination despite oppression. Unwitting, they endured the sulfurous flames of a cruel history together!

Dolittle looked on them with a sense of long-neglected pride. His ebon neighbors were poor and poorly educated. They had begun their journey in the rotten, plague-infested, overstuffed bellies of schooners and galleys bound from

Africa: La Amistad, The Clotida, Brookes, The São José Paquete Africa, The Whydah, The Jesus of Lübeck, The Henrietta Marie and The Trouvadore among others. Yet despite their status as chattel, or property, they had overcome 400 years of chains in their struggle to stand and boldly peer into the eyes of Justice.

"They still have no idea what they're up against," Dolittle said, shaking his head. "If they knew, they'd be overwhelmed. They'd quit on the spot and go home."

"Even a broken, cold hovel is a home when it's all you got," the First Haint said. "It was a beginning and an end, which marked a *new* beginning."

"I do not want to see it," Dolittle objected. "I do not want to re-live that past."

"If you bury a memory beneath a mountain, it will sing out from the mountaintop. Do you recognize the young man?"

A conflict-ridden black teenager, satchel-full of books, hesitated as he looked down the road. A modest white cinderblock home came into focus, and the more the teenager stared at it, the farther it seemed to move from him. He turned away.

"I can't go back there," Dolittle sighed, "no, not yet." He re-trained his eyes on the intersection signage in the distance: 'Acquiescence at Protest.' "Now I remember that road, that choice," he said.

"And you chose?" the First Haint asked.

"Not actually," Dolittle answered, shaking his head. "It was my destiny. In the early 1960s, I had little choice but to follow the path of protest, but it was nothing new. Dr. King and others introduced it on the greater world stage a decade earlier, but that intersection defined even *your* place in history."

"It was nothing new, even in my time," the First Haint nodded. "Before me, there was protest dating back to the Fugitive Slave Act of 1793, which prevented free blacks from being captured in the North and sold into slavery in the South."

"Then let us not forget Dred Scott v. Sandford, in 1857!" Dolittle interrupted, "the landmark case in which the Supreme Court held that 'the U.S. Constitution was not meant to include American Citizenship for black people, whether they were enslaved or free. The Court ruled that the rights and privileges that the Constitution conferred upon American citizens did not *apply* to black persons, or whatever they were back then—not according to the intentions of the Founding Fathers.'"

"Damn small-minded bigots! My parents remembered Scott!" the First Haint recalled. "He protested in the only way he knew how. After his 'owners' took him from Missouri up to the *Missouri Territory*, where 'Negros' were considered 'free,' he sued the Missouri court and argued, protesting that he had 'automatically been freed' by travelling there, and he and his wife were no longer legally slaves, according to the Missouri Compromise…"

"Yeah, but that U.S. Supreme Court decision went 7-2 *against* Dred Scott," Dolittle recited by rote, "ruling that blacks were not included, and beyond that, were not *intended* to be included under the word 'citizens' in the Constitution. Therefore, blacks could not claim any rights of privileges which that instrument provided for and secured to citizens of the United States."

"Non-citizens, non-persons," the First Haint fumed. "*Merde, pauvre homme! Merde le plus sale!* We weren't even human! We were considered no more than property to be owned," it continued, "and America's greatest legal minds found rationalization to justify that past injustice, though little has changed since then, even in the present, *n'est-ce pas?* The Court has conditioned America's judges and the American justice system—the colored and the women among them—to think and adjudicate like obstinate old white men whose time passed in 1857."

"I fought against injustice in my past," Dolittle insisted. "I remember it more clearly now. I was a member…"

"You are our reluctant legatee! To you, my name has been no more than a title in a landmark case, Thomas, and all the more with Dred Scott. Yet see you here the man!"

In that moment they appeared, as shadows unseen, standing in a room behind a table where Etheldred and Harriet Scott were seated, poring over a document amid intense discussion.

"C'ain't nobody see it?" Harriet said, "or do they see only what they wanna see? We was free, livin in free states—Illinois, Fort Snelling, the Wisconsin Territory. We was married by a Justice of the Peace, somethin no slaves could ever do? Our girls was born free, in *free* territory! Then Emerson move us down here ta Missouri, and we slaves again?"

"I just come back from Miz Irene Emerson house," Dred explained. "Bein Mr. Emerson dead, I told her I would give up $300 ta buy freedom for me and you and the girls, but she said 'no.' She wanna keep hirin us out."

"How, after anyone get the smell of what freedom is," Harriet wept, "how could they evva abide the life of slave fa theyselves, and fa they daughters?"

"There, there," Dred comforted. "America aspires ta be built on laws and principles—ideals that hold even the President into account. When we can't find justice from those who make the law and those who enforce the law, then we gotta find it from the courts, who have the final say to what law is."

"But they sayin law don't apply to us cuz we somethin *less* than them," she said. "Thomas Jefferson say all mens is created equal."

"Jefferson never saw us as men or persons," Dred sighed. "We was mules, we was horses and wagons. It never crossed his mind that a mule or a wagon or plow could ever think to be free."

"I spect justice got no meanin ta white folks," Harriet nodded, "when it ain't them bein hurt or sold. They'll sell our daughters away from us—we'll never see em again!"

"We won our case in court in 1850," he insisted. "Once free, always free. We all free now!"

"Nah," Harriet hissed, "in some places we will nevva be free! There is one of *two things I have a right to, liberty or death. If I can't have one, I'll have the other.*"

Stepping out from the darkness, the First Haint shook his head. "That victory was temporary. Two years later, in 1852, the Missouri Supreme Court struck down the lower court's ruling: Missouri no longer had to defer to the laws of free states, overturning 28 years of precedent. The Scotts became slaves again, slaves of Irene Emerson's brother, John Sanford."

"I remember the landmark ruling from 1857," Dolittle said. "The majority opinion was delivered by Chief Justice Roger B. Taney. Taney ruled that any person descended from Africans, whether slave or free, was *not* a citizen of the United States, according to the U.S. Constitution. Further, Taney insisted that freedom or citizenship in the Northwest Territory could not be conferred on non-white individuals, and it voided provisions of the Missouri Compromise for trying to impart freedom and citizenship to non-white persons."

"*Suprémacie blanche! Sacrebleu!*" the First Haint exclaimed. "The Scotts were the classic representation of winning the battle but losing the war. In that same year, Irene Emerson deeded the Scott family to Taylor Blow, one of the abolitionist children of his original owner, who immediately manumitted, or freed Scott and his family."

"I never knew what became of Scott after the ruling," Dolittle said. "A good ending. I suppose all's well that ends well."

The First Haint groaned and took a kerchief from his pocket. Holding up the spectacles taken from Dolittle's nightstand, he cleaned the lenses and handed them back to the confused judge.

"Within a year of briefly tasting sweet freedom," it said, "Etheldred Scott tasted a bitter tuberculosis death. Rather than joy, he endured a lifetime of helplessness and injustice, born in despair, dead in discontent.

Still seated at the table with Harriet, Dred shook his head. "What does it matter if we—only one family, got our freedom, when the majority of negroes are still slaves?"

"Will we nevva be true citizens?" she asked. "I heard about a slave rebellion in Virginia just yestidy. Now they passin laws that Negroes who learn ta read and understand the meanin and power of words is dangerous, but Nat Turner was no fool. We need mo folks like him."

"How melodramatic!" Dolittle scoffed. "The Dred Scott decision was nullified within eight years after the Civil War," he argued. "The Thirteenth Amendment abolished slavery, and the Fourteenth Amendment defined 'citizenship" as belonging to all persons born or naturalized in the United States. Slavery was over."

"But what of due process?" the First Haint asked. "Nor shall any State deprive any person of life, liberty or process without the due process of law?"

"The Fourteenth Amendment was adopted back in 1868. What of it"? Dolittle asked.

"Does there exist due process even now, according to that there Amendment?" the First Haint pressed, "when law enforcement or those who use the castle doctrine, self-defense or fear as an excuse are held to no account for murdering unarmed black men, black women and unarmed black children?"

"I believe the spirit of due process *does* exist today," Dolittle insisted.

"*Mais non.* That spirit cannot rest on a three-legged chair," the First Haint growled, "when the third leg fails in its purpose, past and present. Unreliable branch. Yet what of equal protection? 'Nor shall any state deny any person within its jurisdiction the equal protection of the laws.'"

"That's subject to a fair interpretation of jurisdiction and a thorough interpretation of the laws," Dolittle countered. "Why else would anyone come in to argue before the Supreme Court?"

"The First Amendment, protecting freedom of speech, freedom of the press and freedom of assembly and the right to petition the government?" the First Haint asked. "Do those sacred rights remain protected by the Fourteenth Amendment in your Court?"

"With provisos, stipulations and reasonable exceptions," Dolittle admitted, "but aye, for the most part."

"Yet has the court of late become the instrument of politics?" the spirit insisted, "with fealty conferred by party appointment? The Court of the past got it wrong according to ignorance and bigotry. Yet a politic court is worse than a bigoted court. The politic court confers fealty over justice and ceases independence. Lady Justice becomes a whore to politicians and disappoints her Fathers."

"We are appointed and confirmed according to our ideologies," Dolittle sneered, "and must hold to those principles described and defended in our Senate trials."

"And no room for growth or learning? A whore who cannot hold her head up is what you have become," the First Haint groaned. "Have you no shame or self-respect?"

In that moment, Dolittle and the First Haint were transported to a future time and place in the past, into a courtroom, barely recognizable.

"That's Chief Justice Earl Warren," Dolittle nodded. "We're in 1954. I expected as much from you."

"The Dred Scott decision in 1857 denied citizenship to blacks," the First Haint said, "but after a bloody Civil War, the Thirteenth and Fourteenth Amendments guaranteed freedom, citizenship, due process and equal protection under the law. My case, Plessy vs. Ferguson in 1896, established segregation in the South and institutionalized white supremacy throughout America, which in irony was the model and beacon for freedom in the modern world."

"So now we're at Topeka, Kansas, Brown vs. the Board of Education," Dolittle nodded, "which challenged the widescale segregation of the Plessy ruling."

"*Eh bien*," muttered the First Haint, "This is a new building, a separate building for the Court, *n'est-ce pas?*"

"The decision to build it was in keeping with the court being an independent, co-equal branch of government," Dolittle explained. "Until 1935, the Supreme Court was convened in the Old Senate Chambers within the Capitol. William Howard Taft was the only person to serve as both U.S. President and Chief Justice of the United States Supreme Court. Having been president, Taft thought the Court deserved better accommodations and procured financing. This building embodied the persona of an independent court."

"On the western *façade*," the First Haint mused, "16 marble neoclassical columns of justice, and beneath the pediment, "Equal Justice Under Law'?"

"It's the spirit of the United States Supreme Court," Dolittle answered.

"And the façade on the East, 16 more marble columns and the words, 'Justice is the Guardian of Liberty'?"

"More the purpose of the Court."

"Today is May 17, 1954," the First Haint revealed. "*Mon Dieu!* Had I lived to 92 years old, I would have witnessed the arguments and the decision in the flesh, yet I was there in spirit."

"You were there?" Dolittle asked. "Here?"

"*Mais bien sûr!*" the First Haint answered. "Here and here…"

Instantly, Dolittle and the First Haint were standing on a grayscale street in a modest colored neighborhood in Topeka. The houses were small and simple, the lawns and fences neatly maintained. It was the first day of classes, so kids were dressed in fine new clothes as their parents walked them along streets to the school.

"In Kansas in 1951, a local public school district refused to enroll the daughter of Mr. Oliver Brown at the school closest to their home because she was black," the First Haint summarized, "which meant she would have to ride a bus to a segregated school a good distance from her family's house. Twelve other black families joined the Browns in a class action federal court lawsuit against the Topeka Board of Education, alleging the policy of segregation was unconstitutional."

"This is beginning to sound repetitive," Dolittle interrupted.

"It should," the First Haint answered. "The U.S. court for the District of Kansas relied on the 1896 decision in Plessy v. Ferguson in a verdict *against* the Browns, affirming that racial segregation in itself did not violate the Equal Protection Clause, if the facilities in question were otherwise equal."

"As I said earlier," Dolittle reaffirmed, "I have always *agreed* with that reasoning. That determination should remain with the states."

"A 'separate but equal' doctrine, as adopted by racist states," the First Haint continued. "In the Kansas case, the district court indeed found the facilities to be comparable. At the time, the NAACP was sponsoring five segregation related cases, which were combined and brought before the U.S. Supreme Court in 1952. The United Auto Workers donated $75,000 to pay for the effort."

"Unsurprising," Dolittle interrupted. "The UAW and their likes have always been on the other side."

As the First Haint led Dolittle past a tree, they stepped into the Great Hall of the U.S. Supreme Court, a resplendent marble chamber, steeped in metaphor and history.

The First of the Three Haints

"It was An American Dilemma," the First Haint continued, *"c'est vrai?* In 1952, the American system of justice was on trial on the world stage, to the extent that America wasn't living up to the spirit of its Constitution and its Bill of Rights. The Court, led by Chief Justice Fred Vinson, vacillated, with justices arguing amongst themselves—on issues from states' rights to judicial activism, and with actual 'enforceability' of the law creating divisions. But when Vinson died in September 1953, President Eisenhower appointed Earl Warren as Chief Justice."

"Right," Dolittle scoffed. "I remember Eisenhower's exact words, He said Warren was 'very definitely a liberal-conservative,' representing 'the kind of political, economic, and social thinking that' Eisenhower believed we needed on the Supreme Court."

"And yet *you* have never encountered Jim Crow, *mon ami*?" the First Haint pursued. *"La vraie merde?"*

"Oh, I met him in Georgia and everywhere else I went," Dolittle answered. "My grandfather knew him well."

"Then you know, of course," the First Haint said, "Jim Crow was not born of the Civil War and Reconstruction, but rather from racism some 25 years later, when white southerners decided to create a legally prescribed, rigidly enforced, state-wide system to *disenfranchise* the citizenship that had been conferred on black folks."

"It was the way things were then," Dolittle answered.

"It was the way whites made them to be," the First Haint countered. "As the passion and causes of the war began to fade, a group of confederate veterans formed a club, purposed to enforce the new black codes in the South. These codes regulated where and how blacks could work, and for how much. With slavery over, they wanted to force us into an alternative indentured servitude, take away our right to vote and control where we lived and where we could go. They also wanted to take our children."

"This 'club of confederate veterans'?" Dolittle asked. "They lost the war, so how could they accomplish all that?"

"Never underestimate the resolution of hate, foolish Thomas. This same club of confederate officers and soldiers," the First Haint answered, "they became the powers—the politicians, judges, lawyers, sheriffs and business owners in the southern states by day—so certainly they had the means to accomplish all that—but they transformed as the Ku Klux Klan in darkness, which sealed the history of the South."

"You're right, my pale guide, but that was nearly a century ago," Dolittle argued.

"They clung to the memory of that past. They are still clinging to the symbols and tenets of oppression and the disenfranchisement of black people, as represented by the Confederate flag, defunct plantations, a coded, dog-whistle language of hate and a nostalgia for another time, when white supremacy held sway unopposed. Thus the black codes!"

"The 'white' and 'colored' drinking fountains then?" Dolittle asked, becoming irritated, shaking his head in recollection. "The seats at the back of the bus, the backdoor fly-infested tables behind the white restaurants, the psychology that reinforced that we were substandard. I remember having to bow my head to avoid looking a white man in the eyes and crossing the street to avoid passing too close to a white woman."

"The Thirteenth Amendment ended institutional slavery," the First Haint continued, "which was transformed to indentured servitude for women in white folks homes for meager wages, and for families in sharecropping, where blacks, like poor whites in the mines, owed their souls to the landlord or the company store. Brown vs. the Board of Education was the opening volley to end those oppressive black codes."

"The unanimous 9-0 decision, which desegregated schools, ultimately ended legal segregation in the South," Dolittle said.

"Though not without great struggle, resistance and duplicity," the First Haint added. "Yet the decision was not an end, but a beginning, which led to the 1964 Civil Rights Act, but that is another story for another haint."

"I recognize that man—that lawyer there," Dolittle said. "I get the feeling that he's somehow related to me."

"You are related more to him than you have imagined," the First Haint said, "to this civil rights lawyer from Baltimore, but you don't see it, not yet. He was the right man in the right place. And you, poor man, a blind judge in a complicated race."

"I see the law, and the country for that matter," Dolittle responded, "as it should be, as it must be. We must elevate to the highest ideals."

"Of whom?" the First Haint asked. "The Founding Fathers?

Dolittle and the haint instantly stood before the stately 1775 Monticello in Virginia.

"Ah, the home of our third president!" Dolittle sighed. "I have always wanted to see this place."

"Poor stepchild," the First Haint said. "Those Founding Fathers would have been relieved to see you and would have thought it proper to see a sturdy nigga like you served 'Derby's dose' or assigned to privy duties. Perhaps you need to feel and smell reality versus the ideal?"

Dolittle and the First Haint sank below earth and stood at the intersection of various tunnels beneath the huge Virginia estate, where the sudden overwhelming stench of raw human sewage invaded Dolittle's nostrils, flooding his mouth and lungs. A vile sludge oozed down crusted, putrid, bubbling, foul, sulfide-stained shafts along open rusted pipes into mushy, turd-soup, over-brimming "earth cars" for eventual burial by an assigned slave, who would earn one dollar a day in payment for his efforts.

"My God!" Dolittle exclaimed, holding his nose, gasping, "What is the purpose of this! Get me out of here, Haint! Now!"

"*Au contraire, mon frère.* To your Founding Fathers, you would have not been very special at all. Accept it. Breathe in the reality and outcomes of their highest ideals!" the First Haint scoffed while handing Dolittle a harness, rope and shovel. "Thirty feet out yonder on that board, you'll dig a pit, six feet deep, and dump that heavy railcar. Then you'll come back to get another."

Another dripping railcar came down the tracks, crashing into the first, spilling the contents onto the front of Dolittle's shirt, causing him to gag and vomit up his earlier-consumed grits.

"No!" Dolittle pleaded. "This is not reality. America's moved beyond this madness!"

"Not for the man and men who worked down here for years," the First Haint said. "He never moved beyond it, and there are still such jobs to be done to support the unreal narratives that you believe," the spirit said as a third car came down the chute. "Generations upon generations of crap! Now get to work, black boy, or face the consequences!"

"No, no!" Dolittle cried. "I'm better than this. I worked hard. I sacrificed. I earned my place!"

"You're yunt, Thomas! That man worked harder than you ever have," the First Haint taunted, "*he* earned your place, you ungrateful fool! Now you will take his. Answer to your lowly privy master!"

Dolittle heard the crack of a whip before he felt the sharp stinging pain on his back and a trail of blood that oozed, his sweaty body becoming suddenly covered with biting flies.

"Move them cars, you smelly, lazy nigguh," the privy master complained, his face resembling one of the many

The First of the Three Haints

largemouth bass fish heads floating in the muck. "Move them full-over cars or you'll get a whuppin instead of your gad-damned dollar!"

"No! Enough, please!" Dolittle relented, begging the First Haint. "I get it. Please get me out of here! I'll listen better now. Just get me out of here, Haint! Take me anyplace but here!"

"You would rather be a judge than work here in waste management?" the First Haint asked.

"Yes! Please!" Dolittle screamed. "I *am* a judge. That is my proper place!"

"Yet what place has a judge?" the First Haint asked. "What duty has a judge?"

"Why," Dolittle said, "the duty of a judge is justice foremost."

"Except when justice itself becomes injustice," the First Haint contested. "Watch yourself, judge!"

This time, the transformation placed Dolittle in a judicial position in the Greenwood District, Tulsa, Oklahoma, the district attorney and opposing counsel arguing angrily. *Black Dispatch* and *Tulsa World* reporters asked questions and wrote furiously on notepads.

"That shoeshine boy, that Dick, that Dick Rowland," one white reporter shouted, "contrary to the suggestion that he *knew* Miss Sarah Page, the elevator operator—there's no question but that his action constitutes a felonious assault. Something must be done! Justice must be served!"

"He was in the building only to use the bathroom on the top floor, which was the only acceptable place where we Negroes could go to relieve ourselves when nature called," a black attorney said. "That was a regular thang. Mr. Rowland knew Miss Page, your Honor. Even *she* don't like this, but she would tell you they were friendly, though certainly not friends. When the elevator jolted, he lost his balance and fell acrost her—never to touch her except to grab her arm momentarily. It wasn't her—it was the clerk who said she was assaulted. She never said that."

"And Mr. Rowland has been arrested?" Dolittle asked.

"Arrested and moved to the main jail," the district attorney answered, "where Sheriff McCullough is trying to hold off a lynch mob, who are demanding him and threatening to take him by force, like they did last year."

"Mark my words," the black attorney said, seeming to grieve as he referenced God in heaven, "this will not end well. On the other side, there's a group of one hundred blacks—seventy-five or so soldiers from the war—armed—who say they won't let the whites take Dick Rowland out and kill him."

"That's already history," a reporter said as he entered the courtroom. "When the whites—by this time over a thousand strong—when they saw that the negroes were armed—they went home and got their guns. The National Guard got involved, confronting the lynch mob, which had swelled to 2,000 armed kluckers."

"A desiccated tinderbox in a flashing summer lightning storm," the district attorney said, "a massacre in the making."

"When some white men attempted to disarm the blacks," the First Haint said, "the first shot was fired—accident or statement—who knows, but it triggered an exchange, killing ten whites and two blacks, and then as they say, 'it was on.' Outnumbered, the blacks involved retreated to Greenwood. A riot was declared."

A nighttime scene emerged, with the National Guard and the American Legion converging to protect the white districts in Greenwood. In the meantime, the armed whites began shooting any blacks that could be found. Members of the lynch mob were deputized by the Greenwood Police and told to "get a gun and kill a nigger."

Scenes of horrific violence followed as irate whites invaded the black Greenwood community, guns drawn,

The First of the Three Haints

firing on black lives—men and women, elderly and children. No one was spared. And then the looting and burning of stores and homes began. It went on through the entire night of May 31, 1921.

As if by design, Dolittle's eyes settled on a home that was familiar in his mind. Three white men kicked down the front door, rushed in and came out, physically restraining an old black man and an old black woman, abusing both before throwing them to the ground on their front lawn.

"No!" Dolittle said to the First Haint. "This isn't fair!" he complained, looking on as his proud grandfather lay injured on the grass, his wife pleading for help. "He was never in Tulsa. This never happened to him!"

"How wrong you are," said the First Haint, "as it was done unto the least of his brothers, it was done unto him... and was done unto you. Somewhere in your life you've ceased to see it, but now you will," it said as two of the men drew rifles, aiming at the old couple.

"No!" Dolittle protested. "I don't want to see it! Please!"

The old man grasped the old woman's hand and looked directly at Dolittle, disgusted. "That there boy ain't no kin ta me," he said to the First Haint, defiant, before shots rang out and his body collapsed in an expanding pool of blood.

"If the duty of a judge is justice," the First Haint asked, "then what judge can ignore or excuse injustice?"

"This was 1921!" Dolittle argued. "I wasn't even born. My mother wasn't even born back then."

"Irrelevant," the First Haint answered. "If you cannot see Injustice Past, then you will never see injustice at all and therefore you will always be derelict in your duty as a judge. Do you believe what happened in Tulsa in 1921 does not reverberate today, and will tomorrow?"

Houses burned in the distance and black people scrambled into the streets in panic as "lawful deputies" shot them indiscriminately.

"They called this the Black Wall Street," the First Haint said, "the wealthiest black community in the United States at that time, and you are witnessing the single worst incidence of racial violence in American history—35 blocks besieged—300 blacks dead, owing to hate and resentment from whites, 800 in hospitals, 6,000 locked up, 10,000 left homeless, millions of dollars in damages—which would be much more now. *Et pourquoi, Monsieur?*

"*Pourquoi?*" Dolittle repeated.

"For what?" the First Haint answered. "It is the power they gave to the word of a young white woman—though in all fairness to Miss Page, she was less complicit, rather than a convenient excuse for others."

"No, this didn't happen!" Dolittle protested.

"Open your eyes, Judge, and consider the cost," the haint said. "Consider what those 300 wealthy murdered blacks could have contributed to the greater community over the 100 years that followed. Consider how that wealth would have grown to empower entrepreneurial black businesses the world over.

"Consider the example, power and inspiration a successful Black Wall Street would have provided over a century of struggle, and then consider the unmistakable message sent in the bloody massacre and its destruction—it was the ultimate *How Dare You!*. And if nothing else, consider the proud, principled men, like your grandfather, who were defiant to the end, faith intact that a change was gonna come."

"My grandfather was never there!" Dolittle complained.

"But he was," the First Haint returned, "in the important ways. Open your eyes, Judge, and see Injustice Past."

"No! I've seen enough! I've seen enough, Haint! Remove me," Dolittle exclaimed. "I cannot bear it. I will see it looking forward! But take me away from here!"

He turned upon the First Haint, and seeing that it looked upon him with a face that in some strange way contained fragments of all the faces it had shown him, he reached over and wrestled with it.

"Leave me. Take me back. Haunt me no longer!"

In the struggle, if that could be called a struggle, in which the Haint, with no visible resistance on its own part was undisturbed by any effort of its adversary. Flailing, Dolittle observed a large scab on the back of the First Haint's swelling head, and thinking that by his removing it, he might abate the growing pressure, he seized the scab and ripped it off.

The First Haint seemed to smile as a foul liquid oozed out, quickly boiling and becoming gas, as the huge head began to shrink, and Dolittle held the head, squeezing hard, demanding to be released, until all the fluid from the head and body were drained, and a deflated, withered ethereal form escaped his grasp and floated upwards toward the heavens.

Dolittle was conscious of being exhausted and overcome by an irresistible drowsiness, and further—of being in his own bedroom. He tossed the withering scab aside, which from his relaxed hand fell, and he had barely time to reel in bed before he sank into a heavy sleep.

SHOUT III

SHOUT III
The Second of The Three Haints

Dolittle was awakened by the snort of one of his own snores, so loud that it caused him to sit erect in his bed, disoriented, hardly recalling the episodes of the journey earlier. As he looked about his room, which he had witnessed in flames in memory, it wasn't a dream—it was something more oracular.

"It's six o'clock a.m." the Virginia app proclaimed. "It's seven o'clock a.m. It's eight o'clock a.m. It's two o'clock p.m.... It's six o'clock p.m...." Thus in rapid succession, day came and moved toward night until... "It's twelve o'clock a.m."

Dolittle realized just then what was in store. "That damn Marshall!" he muttered angrily, his eyes on the LED clock display where the minutes ticked by like seeming seconds. Soon it would be 1:00 a.m. and the Second Haint would arrive.

Fully conscious, he rose from the bed and prepared the room. That First Haint had caught him off-guard and incredulous of the exercise. Injustice Past—Dolittle knew the case history and the spirit of the law, but he had been unprepared for the challenge, especially with the invocation of his grandfather.

That tactic was improperly personal and unfair, so if this next Second Haint's condemnation continued along that tack, the judge would be ready to defend himself and would call out the impropriety and indecency of the ploy.

Dolittle walked down the hallway and opened the door to his personal office, turning on the lights—no spirit lurking in the shadows. Opening a file cabinet, he hauled out the most recent opinions he had written for the court.

He also extracted briefs on a panoply of issues, ranging from abortion and immigration to affirmative action, policing, sentencing, incarceration, the death penalty, environmental, LGBTQ issues and others for good measure. He arranged them according to his expectation of the Second Haint's probable argument strategy, according issues involving race more heft.

The First Haint knew the history of "so-called" injustice, but he was a shoemaker, not a lawyer. If this Second Haint was not prepared for a detailed, logical *legal* debate about injustice, then Dolittle would school him and send him on his way and dare any Third Haint to try him.

There was *Fisher v. University of Texas at Austin*, which centered on whether the University of Texas violated the constitutional rights of some *white* applicants when it used race as a factor in the admissions process.

Or perhaps they would discuss *Citizens United v. Federal Election Commission*, where the court overturned *Austin v. Michigan Chamber of Commerce* and *McConnell v. FEC*, freeing labor unions and corporations to become more actively involved in elections. Or maybe *Home Depot U.S.A. Inc. v. Jackson*? Dolittle was prepared for any question or challenge.

So he sat at his desk, ready for the Second Haint, daring it to appear, when the female voice on the app announced, "It's one o'clock, a.m."

For a moment, it seemed nothing happened. No spirit appeared. Dolittle laughed. *It must be rethinking its appearance—not quite ready for me!*

Yet as he looked about, his office began a transformation. He found himself standing in a dark place that had become freezing cold, pitch blackness surrounding him, and suddenly he felt a suffocating claustrophobia, bordering on fear and an anxiety attack. He felt a heated breath or breeze. Was the hideous Second Haint hovering there someplace just beyond his perception? He thought he heard a dog in the distance. Something sinister was approaching, coming for him?

Then came echoes from a childhood nightmare. Dolittle was fourteen years old, and he was visiting relatives in a strange place. He felt disturbed by something that had happened earlier in the day, an incident where he was wrongfully accused.

He heard the grown-ups talking in worried, frightened voices, and his grandfather, Moses, readying for a confrontation with the angry white men who were certainly coming for him. The story felt ominously familiar, so he decided to make a run for it.

Minutes later, he heard the hounds, saw the torches of the men pursuing him and who were intent on doing him great bodily harm. Distinguishable in sultry moonlight, he ran through the woods and bushes, thorns and snags tearing at his flesh, his legs, arms and face bloodied as he cried out for help in a wilderness.

"Bobo!" a white man called after him. "Where are you, Bobo? We only wanna *talk* to ya, boy."

In the distance, he saw a building with a light in the window, deep in a thicket. If he could only get through the brambles and branches to reach that building. No—it was a church! Surely, he'd be safe there! Hounds baying and furious men's voices close behind, he broke into the clearing before the church.

Now, if he could only reach the door and get inside before the white men caught him! Hearing them break through the briars and thicket, he sprinted across the grass toward the door with all his might, praying they would not catch him.

As he reached the door, it swung open, and when he was safely inside, it slammed shut behind him. Suddenly, it was quiet, but he was alone in the church. When he looked at his arms and legs, the wounds had been healed and he had returned to his proper stature and age. A stage light came on in the distance, and he saw a group of black folks in purple robes, which he recognized as a choir. A seeming child stood in the foreground with a microphone as the song began.

"Well—it's not my sister and it's not my brother, but it's me, Lord."

"Well it's not my momma and it's not my papa, but it's me, Lord..."

When the little person in the front began, Dolittle realized that he was a small man, calling out in a first tenor's voice.

"It's me, it's me, oh Lord—standin in the need of prayer,
It's me, it's me, oh Lord—standin in the need of prayer."

What seemed most remarkable was his shadow, since that diminutive soloist cast an enormous, disproportionate specter of a shadow that nearly obscured the choir, and at one moment, that shadow turned independently to peer upon Dolittle.

"It's not my sister, but it's me, oh Lord, standin in the need of prayer.

It's not my brother, but it's me, oh Lord, standin in the need of prayer."

The shade disappeared as the choir responded.

"Well it's not my uncle, and it's not my cousin, but it's me, Lord.

Well it's not my gramma and it's not my grampa, but it's me, Lord.

It's me, it's me, it's me, oh Lord, It's me, it's me, it's me oh Lord."

The soloist and the huge shape turned toward Dolittle, singing toward him.

"It's me, it's me, oh Lord—standin in the need of prayer,
It's me, it's me, oh Lord—standin in the need of prayer."

"Not my brother," the choir called, "No, it's me, oh Lord," the soloist responded, "standin in the need of prayer," said the choir.

"Not my sister," from the choir, "No, it's me, oh Lord," he answered, "Standin in the need of prayer."

Well it's not my Justice and it's not my lawyer, but it's me, Lord.

And it's not protesters and it's not policemen, but it's me, Lord

It's me, it's me, oh Lord—standin in the need of prayer,

It's me, it's me, oh Lord—standin in the need of prayer."

The choir and the soloist sang together toward a finale.

"It's me, it's me, oh Lord—standin in the need of prayer."

"It's me," he called, halting, *"it's me, oh Lord..."*

The choir responded *a fermata*, and then slowly, building to an end—*"standin... in the need... of prayer!"*

When the song ended, the choir dissolved, and the lights came up, leaving only Dolittle and the soloist in the chamber of a venerable empty courtroom, with tables containing all his written opinions and briefs. The soloist approached Dolittle, its shadow close behind.

"I take it you're the Second Haint," Dolittle observed. "You're not really scary. You're so small."

"I prefer to call it 'humble,'" the haint said calmly.

"But I'm not small or humble," the Shadow interjected.

"No, you are neither," Dolittle said. "Then the question, which one of you is the Second Haint?"

"It's me," the Second Haint said, "and my shadow, Huey—*closer to pages that stick in a book*. He's a progressive nuance that has always followed me. Suffice it to say, you got both of us."

Dolittle looked at the pair in amazement—the small man and the hulking specter. Whereas the First Haint had been pale and deathly white, this haint was definitely brown skinned, with unusually big ears. It seemed to be less sullied by the effects of death than the First Haint, yet Dolittle could hear its Shadow breathing labored breaths, which seemed like menacing breaths.

Dolittle was not imagining things. The Second Haint's Shadow moved independently of the little man, which was unnerving, and it generated icy waves of cold and frost as it moved, especially when its shape fell upon Dolittle's flesh. At one time, Dolittle drew his arm back to find his fingers nearly frostbitten and frozen. Thus avoiding the Shadow, he spoke to the diminutive man.

"You're the Haint of Injustice Present?" Dolittle asked. "Well, I've prepared for you. What have you come to show me?"

"I came to teach a blind man to see," the Second Haint answered.

"But you ain't really blind, black lil nigga," added the Shadow in a bass-baritone. "You just don't *wanna* see."

"I seek to see the *justice* in the law," Dolittle answered, "others seek to see the injustice."

He looked over to a table in the courtroom where his legal opinions, casework and briefs were arranged just as he left them at the table in his office.

"Ah!" he said to the Second Haint. "I take it you'll want to talk about my opinions regarding *injustice* in America? I've laid out my arguments and scholarly opinions on that table over there. Where would you like to start?"

"In the empire," the Second Haint said. "I appreciate all your written legal opinions, prevailing, concurring or in dissent. I've read them, unimpressed, but I, I think we need to go out into the empire for something more. On that table lies the theoretical musings of scholarly though inexperienced old men and old women, often detached from reality."

"We have case law for reality," Dolittle argued.

"Case law does not breathe, it does not bleed," the Second Haint refuted, "it does not suffer the pain, humiliation and bitter frustration of injustice. And last, case law does not die. You stopped understanding empirical reality when you began sipping to intoxication on law and evidence, nine times-distilled by the nature and make-up of the court."

The Second of the Three Haints

"You have a strange, familiar cadence to your voice," Dolittle said. "Do I know you? What is your name?"

"You don't know me," the Second Haint said. "My name is Logos."

"Now that's a blasphemy!" Dolittle warned. "You are not Him!"

"Not *the* Logos, who I believe is within each of us," the Second Haint differed. "Humbly, just Logos, who has come to *know* the Logos."

"What then, about Injustice Present?" Dolittle asked.

"Wax on, wax *off*, Hannibal Thomas!" the Shadow howled, blowing its cold breath, obliterating the table, with all its opinions, cases and rulings to frozen dust that floated away and disappeared. "The *empire* is the streets where we live. It wasn't on that table, but it'll be out there!"

In that moment, Dolittle was transported to a place within a car on a rainy, wintry day. Looking in his rear-view mirror, he saw the cherries and berries of the law enforcement vehicle alternately flashing its headlights.

Jerking abruptly, he tapped the right-turn signal and pulled over to the curb. He immediately took his wallet from his back pocket and removed his drivers' license, placing it on the dashboard. Then, after peeking back nervously, he reached over to the glovebox and retrieved his vehicle registration and the insurance certificate and placed them on the dashboard as he waited, hands on the steering wheel. Something tapped on the window. Glancing back, Dolittle saw a .357-gun barrel pointed at the back of his head.

"Roll your window down, now!" a rude law enforcement officer screamed.

Dolittle spoke as he complied, handing a second cop his driver's license and registration. "What, what did I do, officer?"

"Shut up! Just get out of the car, nigger!"

"No, wait," Dolittle pleaded. "I'm not one of them. I'm a judge. I went to law school."

"I said shut up!" the officer barked. "We gotta report of someone matching your description stealing cigarettes from a liquor store down the street. We're checking it out."

"I don't even smoke," Dolittle insisted.

"Non-compliant!" the officer ruled. "On the ground, now!" Gun holstered, he threatened Dolittle with a large metal black flashlight, tapping it on his thigh, daring Dolittle to disobey.

Dolittle looked from the large rain puddle before him into the arrogant eyes of white supremacy. Slowly, he dropped to his knees, and then he eased face-down into the cold, muddy rain-filled depression, ruining his suit, scarring his soul. He cringed as he felt the pain and pressure of a knee being driven into the small of his back until he wanted to cry out in agony, though he would not as his mouth filled with muddy water.

At once, the officer's face was near his, speaking directly into his ear.

"You're a nigger, and that's all you'll ever be. I don't care where you live, where you work or how much money you make. You'll always be a nigger in my book, and I'm never gonna let you forget that. You got that, nigger?"

Dolittle's refusal to respond only brought greater pressure to his spine. He groaned.

"I didn't hear your answer," the officer said. "I said, 'you *got* that, nigger?'"

Unable to bear the pain any longer, Dolittle hollered out. "Yes, yes!"

Palm on the back of Dolittle's head, the officer pressed the judge's face to the bottom of the muddy puddle, bruising his lip. Face underwater, he heard the men whispering.

"My partner here says it wasn't you," the officer said, tossing the driver's license and registration into the water. "You can go for now, but we'll be *seein* you."

The Second of the Three Haints

As Dolittle rose, he found himself suddenly in the path of the police cruiser speeding toward him, forcing him to dive aside into an even larger ditch.

When he rose again, the Second Haint and the Shadow stood beside him.

"A few bad apples?" the Shadow laughed. "How you like them apples, nigga?"

Spine still throbbing from the abuse, Dolittle gritted his teeth. "That was highly inappropriate. Did either of you get the badge or license plate number? I'll file a complaint."

"Highly inappropriate?" the Shadow mused.

"Inappropriate happens all day, every day across America," the Second Haint said. "In fact, 'Inappropriate' happens so often in cities that it's become standard police procedure. That officer did nothing wrong. You were non-compliant."

"Why? Because I said I didn't smoke?" Dolittle asked.

"You still don't get it," the Shadow sighed. "Your black skin itself is non-compliant."

"Other than your pride," the Second Haint continued, "you remain uninjured. Let's take this to the next level."

Reality dissolved, swirling into a surreal, austere, wintry park scene in Ohio. Dolittle, the Second Haint and the Shadow stood under a tree, remnants of snow covering the grass and decorating shrubs and bushes. A small pre-teen black boy sat at a bench beneath a gazebo, airsoft toy gun before him on a table.

"What the Hell is this?" Dolittle demanded. "What are you trying to prove? Stop this! That boy looks like my *son*!"

"Do you truly believe in the Second Amendment, the right to carry arms'?" the Second Haint asked.

"Of course I do!" Dolittle committed.

"Well, if adults have the right to open carry *real* guns," the Shadow asked, "shouldn't little boys have the right to carry toy guns?"

"Toy guns can *look* like real guns," Dolittle argued.

"And children can look like real adults," the Second Haint said, "but not in this case. He was only twelve. The perceived threat is *not* the toy gun, but the color of his skin."

Dolittle, the Second Haint and the Shadow watched as a police patrol rushed to the scene and officers reached out from the car, guns drawn. The young boy, suddenly afraid, grabbed the toy gun from the table and attempted to hide it in his waistband.

From the boy's point-of-view, the officer was screaming something at him, gun drawn, though in the boy's young, inexperienced mind, he could not understand what the officer was saying or why he seemed so angry. *I'm sorry! I'm afraid!* the boy thought. *I want my mom! Did I do something bad? Do you want me to give you my toy gun?*

The boy approached, complying by taking the toy from his waistband to hand it over, when the officer jumped out of the still-moving car and shot twice center mass within a few seconds of arrival. The twelve-year-old's slight body collapsed immediately, tumbling to the ground.

A fourteen-year-old girl nearby, who was with the boy, heard the shots and immediately rushed to provide aid and comfort to the suffering, bleeding child, but she was tackled by a second officer, handcuffed and threatened to cease her genuine shock and grief. In the meantime, the officers allowed the young boy to lie there in pain, without providing aid.

"That's inhuman," Dolittle said as he witnessed first-hand what bullets do to young black bodies.

"That's at least once a week in America," the Second Haint said. "We don't hear about other incidents because, without social activism and protest, they're never investigated or even reported."

After Dolittle, the Second Haint and the Shadow approached the boy, he looked directly at them.

"Who are you?" the boy asked Dolittle. "Are you my dad?"

"No," Dolittle answered.

"Well, then are you God?" the boy pleaded. "Why did this happen? What did I do wrong?"

"You didn't do nothin wrong, young brotha," the Shadow answered. "You was born black, is all."

The boy cringed in pain and relented, tear-flooded eyes closing before he dissolved into dust, which a gentle breeze carried upward and away.

"And the fate of this little boy?" Dolittle asked.

"He's dead," the Second Haint answered. "And what is the duty of a judge?"

"Justice," Dolittle said. "Surely the officer who shot that child will have to answer for his reckless endangerment that has taken a young life!"

"He was fired by the department for failing to disclose on his application that another city's police department deemed him "emotionally unstable" and "unfit for duty.""

"That's another matter altogether!" Dolittle sighed. "Surely there was an investigation. There were people who witnessed it like we just did. Tell me—was this officer made to stand to account for taking a life?"

"His actions in that incident were reviewed by a retired FBI agent," the Second Haint answered, "who concluded that the killing of that young boy we saw was 'a *reasonable* response' by the officer."

"That's yunt!" Dolittle groaned, "definitely not reasonable!"

"You were there, Judge, but ya didn't wanna *see* it," the Shadow insisted, "and ya *wonder* why folks are protestin!"

"In the first case," the Second Haint offered, "the officer's actions were 'inappropriate.' In this case, they were ruled 'reasonable,' lowering the threshold for devaluing the lives of black men, women and children, making it easier to justify what is prevalent and 'criminal.' How long can America turn a blind eye?"

The scene was transformed so that Dolittle, the Second Haint and the Shadow were standing outside a supermarket, watching as a young black couple with a little girl exited and loaded bags into their car.

"Getting a haircut and a trip to the grocery store shouldn't be a life-or-death gamble," the Second Haint said, "but when there's no accountability for killing black people, it's a toss-up."

"Exaggeration!" Dolittle groaned. "Things aren't as bad as you make them. Our police don't kill people *just* because they're black! In the end, there's always a *justifiable* reason."

"Does the Second Amendment, the right to bear arms, apply equally to blacks and whites?" the Second Haint asked.

"Of *course* it does," Dolittle answered, "according to the Fourteenth Amendment's Equal Protection Clause."

"Is that Second Amendment and the Equal Protection Clause a safe bet for a black man in America?" the Second Haint continued.

"All three branches of government concur and insure it," Dolittle answered. "We're a nation predicated on the 'rule of law.'"

"Would you bet your life on it?" the Second Haint asked.

"Why, yes!" insisted Dolittle.

"Open carry for a black man is dangerous at best," the Second Haint countered. "Black men bet their lives when they open carry."

"*The first lesson a revolutionary must learn,*" the Shadow thundered, "*is that he is a doomed man!*"

The Second Haint waved its hand, and suddenly they were standing in the middle of a traffic intersection. When Dolittle turned toward the sound of a horn growing louder, a truck sped toward him. Eyes widened and too frightened to scream, he braced for impact, but the truck passed right through him.

"Are you afraid of shadows?" the Second Haint laughed.

"Are *we* shadows?" Dolittle asked.

"The good you can do is limited to the time when you can *cast* a shadow," the Second Haint said, "though even when you're gone, your shadow is forever a shade."

"This doesn't make any sense!" Dolittle complained as a shiny grey car passed through him.

"We're standing in the shadow of the past present," the Second Haint explained. "In this place, we are able to witness everything that has ever happened, without touching or changing anything."

"Why here?" Dolittle asked, glancing toward the fairgrounds.

"Listen!" the hidden Shadow growled.

The focus shifted to two officers in a squad car, slowly following a white car."

"That's the family from the supermarket!" Dolittle remembered.

"Just headed home after a shopping trip," it answered.

One of the officers grabbed the com.

"We're gonna be pulling over a white, a white Olds—looks like an Eighty-eight. ID check. The two occupants just *look* like people that were involved in a robbery. The driver looks more like one of our suspects, just because of the wide-set nose. I couldn't get a good look at the passenger."

"Go ahead," the voice on the intercom responded.

The officer flicked the car's high-beams and engaged the flashing lights atop the car. The white Oldsmobile slowed and pulled over to the curb on the right side of the road. The officer approached the car from one side as another officer approached on the other side.

The driver had rolled his window down and was waiting on instructions. Peering inside the car, the officer saw a young female in the passenger seat (not a match for the second suspect in the robbery), and a pre-school child in the back seat (definitely not a suspect).

"Why did you pull me over?" the young black man asked, respectfully.

"I'm going to need to see your driver's license, registration and proof of insurance," the officer responded.

Prepared for the officer's demands, the driver handed over the "proof of insurance" card, which the officer glanced at and tucked in his pocket.

Confident in the rule of law in America and the decency of law enforcement, the young, naïve black man believed full disclosure was the best policy.

"Sir, I have to tell you that I *do* have a firearm on me, because I'm licensed to carry. I'm wearing this seatbelt, but my wallet is in my back pocket. I'll need to retrieve it in order to get my driver's license for you."

The panic from the officer was instantaneous and alarming. He immediately unholstered his gun. His face was sweaty, and his eyes were wild.

"Okay, don't reach for it, then..." he gasped, "don't pull it out!"

Nervous, though still calm, the driver responded, "I'm not pulling it out."

"He's not pulling it out!" the female passenger screamed, terrified.

"Don't move!" the officer demanded.

The driver halted, raising his hands in response.

"Don't pull it out!" the panicked officer yelled as he drew his gun, stuck it in the window and began firing (four-year-old in the back seat) ... seven times at point-blank range!

When the shocking, deafening sounds of gunshots faded in his ears, he looked into the car to witness the destruction. Five of his bullets had pierced the young man's body, two directly through his heart. The interior of the car—as well as the passenger and the child—were covered with blood.

"You just killed my boyfriend!" the female passenger shrieked.

The Second of the Three Haints

Struggling, the mortally wounded man raised his head and opened his eyes, looking directly into those of the officer, almost pleading.

"I wasn't reaching for it…"

And then the loud condemnation from the passenger. "He wasn't reaching for it!"

"Don't pull it out!" the officer screamed, the weight of the event beginning to smother, mock and chastise him.

"He wasn't!" she screamed.

"Don't move!" he responded, his spooked pupils dilated. "*Dammit!*"

"You shot four bullets into him, sir!" the female passenger yelled. "He was just getting his license and registration, sir!"

"I told him not to reach for it!" the officer repeated to himself. "*Dammit!*"

Outside the car, another officer screamed at the female passenger. "Get on your knees!"

As the handcuffs clicked and the woman fell to the ground on her face, she could hear the terrified words of her four-year-old daughter.

"Mom! Please stop cussin and screamin—cuz I don't want you to get shooted!"

In that moment, the entire scene and the people in it dissolved to dust and settled onto the street.

"You insisted you were not blind," the Second Haint said to Dolittle. "Did you see *this* one?"

"I knew of it," Dolittle answered.

"But did you *see* it? Were the eyes of justice blind, though not in justice, but injustice?" the Second Haint asked.

"It was unfortunate," Dolittle said, shaking his head.

"'Unfortunate' happens every day to black people, if you're not blind, Judge," the Second Haint argued. "Was there justice for that young man?"

"I would imagine so," Dolittle answered. "What defense could the officer offer?"

When the Second Haint turned away, it and Dolittle were standing in a courthouse, listening to testimony. The officer was explaining his actions.

"I smelled *marijuana*, and I thought I was gonna die, and I thought if he's, if he has the, the guts and the audacity to smoke marijuana in front of the five-year-old girl and risk her lungs and risk her life by giving her secondhand smoke—and the front seat passenger doing the same thing—then what, what care does he give about me?"

"That's a ridiculous justification," Dolittle sighed.

"It was enough," the Second Haint said. "The officer was ultimately charged with second-degree manslaughter and faced up to 10 years in prison. It was a test for black folk. In this, one of the most egregious of cases, would they finally get justice?"

"How could it be otherwise? The driver did nothing wrong," Dolittle said.

"According to justice in America, the *officer* did nothing wrong," the Second Haint responded. "The officer was acquitted, as did officers killing unarmed black people in case after case."

Dolittle and the Second Haint were back in a courtroom, staring at the jury box as verdicts were rendered.

"We, the jury, find the defendants 'not guilty,'" said a thin, mousy, grey-haired woman.

"The jury finds the defendant 'not guilty,'" a millennial male read from a page.

"The district attorney has found insufficient evidence in this case," a judge said, "to proceed to trial."

"The jury is deadlocked," another judge said. "A mistrial is declared."

"The court finds that the actions of the officers were 'reasonable' in the incident that led to this unfortunate death," a magistrate ruled.

The Shadow howled in anger and puffed a gale toward the jury box, freezing the scene with all its elements, before blowing it away as powdery snow.

"One must only *look* to notice what's happening here, Judge," the Second Haint said. "Rule of law? Do the laws and courts and judges provide equal justice?"

"I... I would say they *do* in most cases," Dolittle answered.

"Why don't you want to recognize it?" the Second Haint asked, and then he turned toward the Shadow. "Load the next scene, will you?"

"Next scene?" Dolittle protested. "No, I've seen enough! No more!"

No sooner had the words been spoken, Dolittle found himself in the driver's seat of an SUV. The sound of something hard tapping on the window at his left startled him. He glanced over to see a worked-up police officer with a flashlight, who rapped on the window again.

"Show me your hands!" the officer screamed.

"Oh Lord!" Dolittle said to himself. "Where am I *now*?"

He opened the vehicle door rather than rolling down the window, intent on assuring the officer that he had done nothing wrong.

"I'm sorry, officer, but I'm sure there's been a misunderstanding…"

"Show me your hands, now!"

"You don't understand," Dolittle protested.

"I said, *show me your hands!*"

"But I…"

The officer immediately drew his gun and pointed it at Dolittle.

"Show me your hands. This is your last warning!"

After Dolittle raised his hands, the officer holstered his gun and put hands on the judge, a personal affront that Dolittle initially resisted. Conceding, he relented, allowing the officer to drag him from the car before handcuffing him.

The officer took Dolittle to the wall of a building and sat him down on his butt, still restrained.

Minutes later, the officer returned.

"You need to tell me the truth," he said. "Are you 'on' something?"

"Really?" Dolittle sighed, disgusted. "No! Why would you ask me that?"

"Well, you were acting very erratic back at your SUV."

"I was terrified," Dolittle answered. "What would you expect? I've seen what you guys do."

"What about the foam around your mouth?" a second officer asked.

"What?" Dolittle answered, wiping. "I just woke up, or maybe I'm still dreaming."

"We'll be back," the first officer said.

"Thank you," Dolittle responded politely.

A few minutes later, the officers returned.

"We're placing you under arrest," one said, "We're taking you to put you in the police car across the street."

The officers stood Dolittle up and began dragging him toward the squad car in the distance. However, the nearer the car drew, the greater Dolittle's anxiety increased. The vision of the car took on the appearance of a black hole. There was something *ominous* about it, sitting there, as he looked at it.

Overwhelmed, Dolittle collapsed at the car door, paralyzed by fear. He felt premonitions of his own death in or near that car. He struggled as the officers lifted him to his feet and pinned him against the car door.

"We need you to get in the car!" one of the officers yelled.

"No, please!" Dolittle protested. "No, I'm claustrophobic! I can't sit in there. I have anxiety!"

"I don't care! Get in the car!" the officer insisted, slamming Dolittle's back against the door to give heft to the threat.

"No! I can't breathe!" Dolittle pleaded. "I'll die in there. Please— let me just lie on the ground here. Please!"

By that time, two additional officers arrived: the first an arrogant man who had a tint of color; and the second a little man with a huge, oversized, menacing shadow.

Now four-against-one, the little man with the huge shadow took charge. He opened the rear door on the passenger side of the car, and after the other officers held Dolittle in the rear door of the driver side, he and the shadow dragged handcuffed Dolittle onto the back seat.

"I can't breathe!" Dolittle gasped, hyperventilating, thrashing about. "I don't wanna be in here! I'll *die* in here! I can't breathe!"

He began an anxiety attack, whipping his arms and slamming his head until his mouth began to bleed. When an officer opened the car door to better subdue him, Dolittle lurched out and crashed onto the street next to the car.

His chest and cheek on the pavement, Dolittle felt the growing pressure from a knee, placed at the back of his neck. It had to be the little man, because Dolittle could see the sadistic shadow he cast, hovering over the little man, blocking out all light, a smothering presence.

"Please! I can't breathe!"

Then he felt the pressure from a second officer, bearing down on his back, and he felt a third, pressing down his legs. He tried to breathe, but all air had vanished with the light. His lungs were on fire, straining to expand under such an immense burden. In the darkness, the knee was the center of gravity, draining his life.

"Relax," the little man said, before bearing down with even more weight.

"Please! You're killing me!" Dolittle pleaded. "Don't kill me!"

He felt the excruciating pain at the back of his neck, in the pit of his stomach and throughout his body. His nose bled, while in agony, he felt extreme thirst.

In darkness, he could hear a crowd gathered around and comments from witnesses.

"He's bleeding! Get off him!" one person said.

"Get your knee off his neck!" another said, "he's not even resisting now. You're *killing* him!"

"He's fine," the slightly colored officer answered, calling out to the crowd. "This is why you don't do drugs, kids!"

Dolittle felt dizzy as his life continued to drain. The scene around him became cold and ethereal. Opening his eyes, he could see the Second Haint, standing in the distance.

"Arise, Thomas," the Second Haint said. "Stand up and come over here. This was but one of my lessons for you on empathy. Rise"

When Dolittle rose, the inert body of a black man rested in his place, unmoving, unbreathing, and yet the little man and shadow continued to torment what was left of him.

Pain and anxiety immediately dissipating, Dolittle looked back at the lifeless body as he approached the Second Haint.

"That was horrible!" he said. "Please don't put me through that again."

"That's every day in America!" the Shadow scolded. "It happens today, tomorrow and every other day!"

Dolittle glanced on the scene a final time, where the little man still had his knee on the black man's neck. "I've seen enough!" he sighed, tears swelling in his eyes. "I know how this story ends."

"Was *that* 'injustice,' Judge?" the Second Haint asked, "or was it 'inappropriate,' or 'unfortunate' or a 'tragedy'?"

"All four!" Dolittle insisted.

"But that big black buck was resisting arrest, wasn't he?" the Second Haint argued.

"It was four against one," Dolittle said. "The remedy for resisting arrest should never be murder, regardless of the circumstances. That was way beyond inappropriate, way beyond a tragedy— it was 'criminal'!"

"Only when it involves you," the Shadow interjected.

The Second of the Three Haints

"That man knew the reputation of law enforcement," the Second Haint added. "He knew his life didn't matter, so he should have just done what they told him to do."

"The man who was pulled over in the *last* scene did just that," Dolittle countered, "and that cop shot him anyway. There's really no justice for you when you're dead. What was this man's name?"

"Legion," the Second Haint answered, "since there will be another like next week or next month, and many, many others in the years that will follow. He'll just have different names. Yet *this* man," the haint continued, "who you just left lying in the street—he had drugs in his system, and he was accused of stealing twenty dollars!"

"The duty of law enforcement is to *arrest* and provide for due process," Dolittle answered. "They completely abridged due process and performed a vigilante execution. That was a criminal act, and justice must be served."

"So how do we get there, Judge?" the Second Haint asked. "How do we get to the place where black victims of crimes receive equal protection and equal justice under the law? Where does the inequity lie? In the laws themselves?"

"I don't see how," Dolittle argued. "Laws are laws, and they should be applied with consistency in jurisdictions across the country."

"And when there is no equal justice," the Second Haint posited, "because there appears to be two separate systems of justice in America, *then* where does the inequity lie?"

Dolittle hesitated, thinking. Reluctantly, he answered.

"Well, I suppose I have to say the final and most frustrating inequity lies in the judicial system, though there's sufficient blame to go around to implicate the executive and legislative branches as well."

"Yet if your *duty* is justice," the Second Haint asked, "then why am *I* here? Why does Injustice Present exist?"

"Because the law's an ass," Dolittle answered, "obstinate and stubborn, slow to act, even slower to change."

"I argue that Justice is this ass's *master*," the Second Haint differed, "and this master is alive and accountable, with eyes that see, ears that hear, a hand that acts, a heart that feels, a mind that understands and blood, which bestows humanity on the master."

"You suggest then," Dolittle pondered, "that Justice has a corporal body?"

"Justice Present *is* a ponderous body, critical in effect," the Second Haint answered. "Justice Present is eyes that are capable of profound sight and insight, but cannot see when her progeny professes blindness, while perceiving, flirting and winking at injustice. Sight is awareness."

"You see in white and black," the judge scoffed. "I see in conservative and liberal. Nuanced vision is critical to sight."

"You don't see at all!" came a deep, booming response from Huey.

"You judge me," Dolittle complained, "if you think I am unaware of what's happening to black lives out there. You don't have to show me another ugly scene. I do perceive injustice, but protest and public wailing are not the answer. Life is personal. The black mindset must be changed at last."

"The 'black *mindset*' must be addressed?" the Second Haint asked, "and not the strong and violent *hand* of the law, unrestrained by its master, gun or club at the ready? Better to address the *ears* of Justice, when she hears but does not act?"

"Justice cannot be rash or act impulsively," Dolittle countered, "but she must listen to the long debate, weighing all matters in the balance of a long arc. She cannot quickly change course, and she cannot provide instant gratification, no matter how loud, popular or angry the protest."

"Then you and others are convinced that Justice is without a heart," the Second Haint sighed, "when natural law is hardwired in the hearts of humans and springs from there. Within the human heart lies the *core* of justice and morality, if you would only search for it there, rather than in artificial and untethered values, conservative and liberal."

The Second of the Three Haints

"That is not the *mind* of Justice," Dolittle said, "but more to the *purpose* of the law, which involves establishing standards, maintaining order, resolving disputes and protecting liberties and rights."

"The purpose *is* the mind of Justice," the haint countered. "Shall we travel to another scene, Judge Dolittle? Or can you apply the *mind* of Justice to the scenes we previously visited?"

"No more of those scenes!" the judge snapped, his complexion becoming chalky. "I don't want to see any of that again!"

"The *blood* of Justice, which is Injustice, makes you queasy?" the haint asked. "The sense of humanity? Then you must realize that when the people bleed unjustly, then Justice bleeds also."

In that moment, both of Dolittle's ears began to flow with steaming blood, startling the judge, who tried to plug them with panicked trembling fingers. The flow temporarily halted until the force began to build, and then the blood began to spray and mist from pressure-pressed openings in the fleshy digital blockades.

"I don't like the blood!" Dolittle returned, even louder. "You need to stop!" And to the Second Haint: "Make it stop now!"

"I'm a phantom," the Second Haint answered. "I don't have the power to *stop* the blood. Even you, a judge, lacks the power to stop the blood of black lives flowing in the streets altogether, but you can make a difference."

"O? How can you be a haint when you're still alive?" Dolittle argued. "You don't think I *know* who you are! You had the power to stop this, but even *you* failed. You had near imperial power and *you* couldn't do it. What do you expect me to do?"

"I was not a judge. I did what I could in my relative place," the Second Haint answered. "Sometimes it may be necessary for me to step back in to change the course of history, which is my duty. In doing so, I have become the embodiment of Injustice Present, though there will come a day when we'll all be haints. If you want the blood to stop, then *you*, Thomas, must do something, rather than little, or the nothing that you actually do."

"I hold to my standard," the judge retorted, "and if that means some must suffer so that the greater part may prosper, then so be it!"

"See it then, Judge!" the Shadow responded. "You can tightly shut your fleshy eyes, but your soul's eyes gape. They see and know, and your soul must answer for your failure to act! Watch and learn, or rather, learn to *feel*. Now live the experience!"

Dolittle awoke in his bed at his personal home, away from the condo he occupied when the court was in session. *Funny!* he thought, *I don't remember coming home.* But there he was, so he glanced around the room and shut his eyes, savoring the sanctum of the space, of the comfortable bed—he remembered the day he and his wife picked it out. There was not a place on Earth where he felt more secure.

He heard breathing inches away and felt the genuine warmth of a human body next to him. It was his wife, and she was smiling as she slept, probably pleased to have him home. There she slept, his partner in adventure, his conspirator in merriment, the love of his life!

There was no warning, no announcement—only the sound of a loud resonating bang as his door gave way to a battering ram outside, and suddenly he heard heavy footsteps in his house, coming up toward his bedroom—that sacred sanctuary.

"Someone's broke into our home!" his wife whispered in shallow panicked breaths. "I'm scared!"

"I'm concerned too, my dear," Dolittle admitted, "but I will defend us." He opened a drawer next to the bed and took out his Glock-9, and sitting up, he aimed it toward the door.

The Second of the Three Haints 95

"They'll think twice if they know I'm armed. I'll fire a low warning shot."

"Be careful!" his wife insisted, putting space between herself and him. "You live under a different law. Your skin color puts *my* life in jeopardy!"

When the approaching footsteps got too close, Dolittle fired a single warning shot, eliciting a cry from outside the door.

Within seconds, Dolittle's ears were deafened by a cacophony of loud gunshots, over thirty, before bullets began to strike objects around him in the room. To his surprise, he was unharmed, but when he glanced over to check his wife, she was covered with blood—struck by six bullets. As he looked into her eyes, he knew that she knew she was dying, and time was short. Gasping for breath, she could muster one word.

"Why?"

Numbed and angry, he screamed out into the darkness.

"You shot her! You shot my wife! Who the hell are you?"

"Walk backwards!" an officer yelled. "Place your hands on your head and get on your knees! I'll turn this dog loose on you if you don't get on your knees right now!"

Dolittle had called 911 to report the home invasion and assassination, and yet when the police arrived, they charged *him* for shooting a police officer and placed him under harsh arrest.

Police? he thought. Unknown *criminals* had broken into his home and had killed, no—they had murdered his wife! *He* was the one who had called the police!

"How can that be?" he asked his lawyer. "I am clearly more sinned against than sinning. What happened?"

"There's been... There *was* a mix-up, a mistake, a tragedy," the lawyer replied. "It was the execution of a scheduled no-knock warrant, but the police officers raided the wrong house under the wrong circumstances. They say they're sorry."

"Sorry? Wrong house?" Dolittle exclaimed. "My wife is dead! They took her from me! Someone must answer for this injustice! There has to be accountability at some level!"

"It's been unfortunate," the city attorney answered. "That's why the city is prepared to offer you a multi-million-dollar cash settlement, provided that you sign a non-disclosure agreement."

"You know what you can do with your settlement and agreement!" Dolittle fumed. "My wife is dead! I don't want your money! I want *her* back! I demand justice for her life! I demand justice for my loss! And I will fight you nonstop, day and night, until I get it!"

In that moment, the city attorney's face transformed itself into the face of the Second Haint.

"You demand justice, Thomas Dolittle?" the specter asked. "You demand justice from whom? And *who* is the final arbiter of the law? *Who* is charged with ensuring the American people the promise of equal protection under the law? *Who* is the guardian and interpreter of the Constitution?"

"It's you, Haint!" Dolittle groaned. "O! How dare you put me through that experience! Such cruelty! You forced me to endure the horror and grief of losing the love of my life! And for what?"

"That was illumination," the Second Haint answered, "yet you call it *horror*. In your world, your wife is fine, but that's not the case for the tens of thousands of black people who lose the loves of *their* lives—their dreams, their spouses, their children and parents—their very hope—every day, every year. They can't wake from it like you did, because it's *real*. Injustice makes haints of us all."

"How dare you!" Dolittle repeated. "You've made a mockery of my emotions! That was not fair."

"Too close to home?" the Second Haint asked. "Tell me, Judge, how do you *like* it out in the empire?"

"I don't!" Dolittle answered. "I hate you!

"Yet, who am I?" the Second Haint persisted.

"You are..." Dolittle stammered. "You are Injustice Present."

"Yet you have never hated me before now," the Haint explained. "You merely ignored me and accepted me as a lesser of evils. But what if I told you that you were trapped here with me eternally, and for my part, I have episode after episode to show to you, and you will be forced to live each incident in horrific and frustrating detail?"

In that moment, members of a great crowd of haints began to appear out of thin air. There was a tall, thin 17-year-old high school male teenager from Sanford in a hoodie, who was buying Skittles; a 27-year-old male with a moustache from Atlanta, who was sleeping in his car; a 28-year-old black female from Miami with a bob haircut, whose only crime was leaving her front door open; a 22-year-old male from Sacramento with 20 holes in his body and a cell phone in his hand, while standing in his grandmother's backyard.

There was a 26-year-old male from Dallas, while sitting on his sofa, eating ice cream; a 37-year-old male from Baton Rouge, while selling CDs and DVDs outside a store; a 25-year-old male from Baltimore, while riding his bike, before being taken down, brutalized, handcuffed and bounced around in the back of a police van, severing his spine; a 43-year-old father from Staten Island, while selling "loosies" (loose cigarettes).

And there was a 28-year-old male from Brooklyn, while standing in a stairwell; an 18-year-old male from Ferguson, Missouri, while merely walking down the street; a 28-year-old female from Waller County, Texas, who was hanged in a police jail cell while being held after a pretextual traffic stop; a 25-year-old black male from Glynn County, Georgia, who was pursued and shot down while jogging; a 47-year-old man in his garage in Columbus, Ohio, while holding a cell phone, with thousands more behind them, and the crowd growing larger every day. "Say my name!" he heard in a haunting echo.

"What if you had to live through every one of those incidents?" the Second Haint asked. "What if you had to experience every last one of these 'unfortunate' deaths every day for the rest of your life—non-stop, for eternity?"

"No! Please don't haunt me that way!" Dolittle insisted. "That would be Hell! That would be a living Hell for me!"

"It's the living Hell your black brothers and sisters live every day in this country, and when they look toward Justice, what they see is *you*, silent, eyes tightly closed, ears stopped, hand closed in a fist, humanity missing. Why should you *not* be forced to live it like they do? It is the reality of Injustice Present. You have a special place reserved for you in a Hell you are imagining only now. You have not lived up to the promise of your legacy."

As Dolittle looked upon the growing crowd of bleeding or broken black men, women and children surrounding him, he felt an immense, irrepressible weight that began dragging him down, like a chain, to a glowing unforgiving infernal realm, and looking skyward, he realized that the collective spirit of that great crowd had then begun to elevate his former partner. He saw Marshall's Haint as it rose on high, heavy chains dropping off and falling down to the Earth with loud trembling, soul-stirring sounds and ground-shaking tremors.

Only then did Dolittle feel that distinctive inkling that he had felt as a child. He remembered feeling the same at times in the company of his grandfather, who had always reminded him of his better angels, his better self—his family character.

Long before he was a judge, he had been called to a sacred duty—a duty to justice in fulfillment of a dual legacy. Somewhere, he had found himself lost along the way. Only at that moment, standing there with the Second Haint, did he rediscover the sacred virtue of "Grace."

So finally, "Haint—" said Dolittle submissively, "conduct me where you will. I went along with you earlier last night, feeling under compulsion, and in spite of myself, I learned the lesson you were trying to teach me. I have endured two haints, and I went along against my will, seeking to prove myself *just*, rather than to humble myself, to stand outside myself in other shoes and other circumstances. I realize now that I owe a debt to a purpose and a legacy."

"It is not necessary for me to conduct you anywhere," replied the Second Haint. "You've been on a return journey to this place from the very day you left. You have resisted it, but it's been inevitable. Do you know where you are?"

"Yes," said Dolittle, shaking his head, his eyes bowed and welling with tears.

"You've always known that you would have to face him again, someday," the Second Haint said. "There was so much left unsaid, so much you have learned. You knew there would be one last meaningful conversation…"

As a familiar house appeared in the distance, Dolittle batted his misty eyes, attempting to re-focus them, until finally, the front door opened. A tired old black man exited and stepped out onto the porch.

"Do you see him?" the Second Haint asked.

"Yes," Dolittle gasped. "Everything I remember of him…"

"It defies rational thought," the Second Haint admitted, "but when you lie convention aside and accept it, this night will make sense to you, and you will finally understand why old Thoroughgood came to see you."

"I'm not ready for a reckoning," Dolittle protested. "Not yet.

"It's not about being 'not ready,' the Second Haint insisted. "It's now about being '*already*.'"

In that instant, the house became hazy until it slowly vanished into the night. An ancient, ivy-covered, fog enshrouded clock in the distance then began to toll, announcing the midnight hour in Vesper notes.

"All in good time," the Second Haint said as he counted the somber hours as announced by the venerable clock. "My time is short now. You must next be visited by the Haint of Injustice Yet-to-Come."

"No! No!" Dolittle groaned. "No more haints! I've seen quite enough!"

"Quiet, enough! You have denied past injustice, Thomas," the Second Haint pronounced sternly, "and you have ignored injustice in the present, so presently, you must see and understand injustice yet-to-come."

The Second Haint's form began to dissipate as the deep reverberating echo from the twelfth bass-baritone bell of the clock faded in Dolittle's inner ears.

"Comes to you upon this hour the solemn Third Haint, grim in aspect, who is called *Ethos*..."

And then the Second Haint was gone.

SHOUT IV

SHOUT IV
The Last of The Haints

Ethos, the Third Haint, did slowly, gravely, silently approach upon the bell of the first hour. When it came near to Dolittle, he knelt, uneasy, as this haint seemed different than the others before it. Initially, he did not perceive it, as it seemed completely merged with the still and utter darkness of night.

Only when it stirred did the judge distinguish the outline of nighttime objects relative to its dark, hooded garment, absorbing ambient light and exerting a sense of gravity, though when it passed between him and the moon or other sources of illumination, they became invisible behind it. As Dolittle stared into the void of that night, he realized the haint seemed dark, rather than black—a shadow, its fluid, deliberate movements perceptible before a seeming lighter background of pitch-blackness.

Dolittle understood the distinction between "black" and "dark." Black is not the same as dark. He had read it in a scientific journal only days earlier. "Black things" absorb light and energy, but they ultimately *emit* their own light and energy, dependent on their capacity and resultant temperature. "Dark things," however, completely *absorb* all forms of energy and light so that no energy or light ever escapes them. Dark things never give anything back. In darkness, there is a palpable gravity.

Dolittle believed that the dark creature next to him was tall and stately when he sensed its presence, and its mysterious aura filled him with a solemn dread. He knew no more, since the haint neither spoke nor moved.

"I take it you're Ethos, the haint of Injustice Future," Dolittle ventured, "the Haint of Injustice Yet-to-Come…"

The Haint did not look upon him or answer, but it pointed in the distance with its hand, insisting that Dolittle proceed in the direction it indicated.

"You are about to show me shadows of injustice that will happen, though not yet, but this injustice will be a consequential result of the past and present... and there is something I must learn or do," Dolittle continued. "Am I right, Haint?"

Although Dolittle had become accustomed to the appearance and presence of dreadful or strange haints by that time, he feared the silent shape so much that his legs trembled beneath him, and he found that he could hardly stand when he prepared to follow it.

As the stern Third Haint paused a moment, seeming to glance down on Dolittle, the judge imagined he could make out its shifting ethereal form. It was tall, well over nine feet, with the strong, broad shoulders resembling LeBron. A huge cloak draped its body, and when Dolittle looked down, its sandaled feet were raised perhaps six inches above the earth, though it stepped deliberately upon an airy "second surface," rather than *floating* forward. Its head was covered with a shrouded hood that extended beyond its hidden face, though its heated eyes, fixed intently upon him, were like two bright yellowish, smoldering coals.

The Third Haint turned and headed in a southward direction, though nothing lied beyond it but utter blackness. Dolittle followed and was astonished to discover that anytime he was *behind* the haint, everything beyond its form was dark, and yet when he caught up with the specter so that he was beside it or ahead of it, a familiar daytime city appeared in the distance.

Dolittle stopped walking at once and watched the sun and the city disappear again on the other side of the dark creature as he fell behind. Turning back, the haint reached out its spectral hand and pointed in the distance.

"Haint of Injustice Future!" Dolittle exclaimed, "I fear you more than any other spirit who has come before me. But as I know your purpose is to do me good, and as I hope to live and learn the lesson Marshall has called my salvation, I am prepared to seek your instruction, and do it with a thankful heart. Can you hear me? Or do you never speak?"

It gave him no reply. The bony truncated finger was pointed straight ahead.

"That's fine!" said Dolittle. "You lead—I'll follow! Or I will rather walk *beside* you so I can see what lies ahead. I sense your visit might carry a more personal message for me, and a conclusion to this matter. As his final act in purgatory, old Thoroughgood came to make a case for my salvation, his final earthly case. I must hear it through. Lead on, Spirit! Lead me tonight."

The journey was not long, for within an instant, the city sprung up around them so that Dolittle and the haint were walking along familiar avenues. The Capitol Dome appeared at left as Dolittle walked beside the haint on New Jersey Street, where masked persons paced along sidewalks, socially distanced in lines outside restaurants, sat on benches, did their banking and participated in social protests.

With historic city scenes in the background, Dolittle and the Third Haint moved along past outdoor restaurants and groups of people, past monuments and history, until they came upon a group of young black and brown people in a wide circle amid a heated debate. They wore heavy coats and gloves to deny the cold its bite, with each of their breaths and comments accented by billows of mist that rose and quickly dissipated.

Dolittle, still in his robe and pajamas, did not feel the cold at all, though he remembered many a morning at that same corner, enduring the freezing wind blast as it channeled through the buildings. He didn't know why the group had assembled, but he imagined it was for some pointless protest, though he had heard a few of their remarks as he and the Third Haint literally passed through the group,

"I never liked him!" sneered one Latino youth. "*¡Es un racista!*"

"We don't know what was in his heart," a Black woman responded. "I was 'prayin' for him."

"*Prayin* for him?" an older Black man said, incredulous. "That man's done more harm to black folks than the KKK!"

When the Haint stopped next and pointed toward two seeming random people, Dolittle took instant notice and at once remembered who they were.

"Those two came into my office this afternoon," Dolittle said. "That Black man there and that Brown woman—Will, and Esperanza, I remember. Yes, they were soliciting me for support."

With no response coming from the Haint, Dolittle reflected on the conversation in his office that afternoon.

"They were complaining about the numbers of Black and Brown persons in prisons and about policing, about low paying jobs and an uneven playing field… and capital investment for underserved communities," Dolittle reflected thoughtfully. "I turned them away."

After saying those words, Dolittle moved in closer to listen.

"No, I don't know much about what happened," Will said. "I only know he's dead."

"When did he die?" one man in the group asked.

"Last night," Esperanza responded.

"What was the matter with him?" another person asked.

"Well, I heard he had a problem with his heart," Will answered, "a lingering problem, which has finally been resolved, I guess."

"Lord only knows," a third person said. "God put him in that special position and handed him a great responsibility. What happens to our legacy now?"

"It was never *his* in the first place," said Esperanza. "It was *ours*, earned through a *history* in blood. He never appreciated it, selfish *bastardo*! It was the "why" for him being there—his purpose, which he pissed away! He made it about 'him.'"

"He wasn't just selfish," a woman sighed. "His short-sightedness made him an enemy of the people!"

"What people?" a second woman asked.

"*We, the People!*" was the consensus answer.

"I'm glad he's gone," Esperanza responded. "Now our people can move forward again. It's incomprehensible what he's already cost us!"

When the Third Haint turned his back to move to the next scene, all light and energy ceased, and Dolittle found himself stumbling, groping, without direction, in utter darkness. A sense of gravity helped him re-locate the Haint. It was only after he caught up and stood beside the specter, looking forward, that the city, the sun and humanity returned.

Dolittle recognized the Southeast D.C. streets and buildings as they came upon the intersection of D and 19th. There was a cluster of concrete and glass buildings that Dolittle recognized as the D.C. Jail. *Why the jail?* he thought as he walked next to the Haint, *and what was the business with the group of people they had passed through?* They were obviously talking about the death of some powerful, prominent person—someone who was not well thought of by that particular crowd.

Dolittle was, he remembered, in the presence of the Haint of Injustice Yet-to-Come, so he concluded the crowd was referring to the future death of some disliked leader or politician. The young Latino man had called the decedent a "racist." *Perhaps,* Dolittle thought, *they were talking about the future death of the former president.*

"Why are we in front of the jail?" Dolittle asked, though futilely. "What business have I here?"

Silently, the Third Haint moved forward, past the "Central Detention Facility" lettering at the entrance, past the guards and magnetometer, beyond the lobby, upward through elevator chutes (and elevators!) and down a corridor and into a cafeteria full of men (mostly Black) in orange pants and shirts.

"I still don't understand," Dolittle insisted. "Why here?"

The Haint continued forward, through the prisoners, who were eating and involved in various conversations. One man sat weeping, with his face in his palms, body quivering. Finally, Ethos stopped next to a group of four young men, extending his arm to point at them.

"What?" Dolittle asked. "I don't know them. I've never seen them before in my life."

Slowly, his mind began to put a series of recent memories of faces in context.

"No, I see it now. You're right!" he admitted. "I *have* seen three of those boys before. They were outside my office last night, singing some blasted, ridiculous song, disturbing my peace! I called the police. You mean to tell me they got locked up?"

The answer to his question was obvious. He sighed and drew closer to discern what they were discussing.

"That was never my complete purpose," Dolittle said, wagging his head in uncommon regret. "I did not want to hear them."

"What're *y'all* all locked up for?" the fourth youth asked the others at the table.

"We got 'got' on a humbug!" Malcom sighed. "That Uncle Tom/Uncle Remus last night, he was once again tryin ta prove ta his white *massas* he's one of the traitorous 'good' niggas at they disposal!"

"We were exercising our constitutionally-guaranteed First Amendment right to free speech," Martin added, "We were demanding change, complaining about public executions of unarmed Black men, women and children by law enforcement, which has become *normalized* in America."

"We got in some *good trouble*," the younger John laughed. "In times like these, our wrongful persecution is a badge of honor."

"They got me for lootin," the nameless fourth rapper youth admitted, "and yeah, I did it, but what else do I got?

When I was eighteen, they charged me for a fake felony, for defendin myself when I got jumped by a group of racists at a party for havin a white girlfriend. I couldn't afford a lawyer, so I caught a felony, and the only jobs I been able to get pay minimum wage—when I'm tryin ta raise a family. When Covid hit, I lost even that, thanks ta that *fool* ova there comparing himself ta Lincoln!"

"Every person must decide on the protest that best suits his or her convictions," Martin countered, "and we all must protest, but looting is *not* protesting. It puts individual gain over collective need."

"What does that even mean?" the nameless rapper complained. "White folks was lootin too, with the PPP, the grants and loans. No one called *them* out. The big corporations and RWP—they took the government for millions, probably billions. All I got was a TV."

"What you got is *arrested*, my brother," Martin said, "and by doing so, you provide legitimacy to those who would discredit our argument and movement. There is a moral imperative at work in our dynamic. *We cannot enlist other persons of goodwill to our cause if we do not hold ourselves to ethical principles.*"

"When *they* don't—" the nameless rapper protested.

"That is the difference between activism and a self-serving reaction," Martin asserted. "Our actions should never be based on what someone *else* does, but on who *we* are and the *principles* we are willing to sacrifice our bodies for... and lives for."

"That takes too long, and who knows if it works!" Nameless insisted. "Nothin's gonna change fa us. That's why we gotta get *ours*, like they be doin."

"When a personal motive is the basis of your response to injustice," Martin answered, "your complaints, however sincere or painful felt, ring hollow, and will enlist little support from others."

"Until we reach a truly race-neutral and classless society, brother Martin," Malcom differed. "then the only option afforded us is to resist, and if that involves *not* looting—but a violent rebellion—we must only look to the revolution that brought about the American experiment in the first place."

"I don't believe what I'm hearing," Dolittle said, unseen, unheard. "Those three were ignorant thugs on my sidewalk, nothing more. This is fake commentary! They don't have the wherewithal or education to even *articulate* such thoughts!"

A mocking silence was all the answer Dolittle received.

"What is your problem with 'individualism'?" he called out to Martin, as if he could be heard.

To Dolittle's astonishment, Martin looked back toward him and answered.

"Despite the determination to unselfishly protest against injustice, I accept that life is personal, Thomas," Martin answered. "But you—worse than being self-centered, Judge, worse than being a great disappointment to your legacy, your family and your race, you have become an enemy, a betrayer of justice."

"That's your opinion," Dolittle responded. "I worked my butt off, and I got over. With your education and platform, you should have gotten over too! You were a fool, but who cares, because you're dead!"

"We *all* will be dead," Martin answered.

In that moment, two armed, uniformed guards approached the door and tapped on it before pushing it open. One read from a document, while the other approached.

"Martin, Malcom and John?" he called. "Good news for you. The person who lodged the complaint against you? As it turns out, he is no longer in a position to *press* that claim."

"Why? What happened?" Martin asked.

"Guess it was his heart," the guard answered. "Too bad for him."

"Heart?" Dolittle exclaimed. "My *heart*! There's nothing wrong with my heart! Or should I be worried?"

"The Lord works in mysterious ways," John said. "What does that mean for us?"

"Where do we go from here?" Martin echoed.

"Well," the guard answered, "the U.S. Attorney for the District of Colombia says that, if nothing else changes, we gotta let you go, immediately."

Martin, Malcolm and John stood and hugged, celebrating beside the table.

"So we must return to our separate lives, my brothers," Martin said, "to provide examples, serve our legacies and leave a better world in our wake."

"You're welcome to go with one of us, brotha" Malcolm said to Nameless.

"Maybe I will," Nameless answered. "Maybe I'll go with all three of y'all. I'll let cha know."

When the Fourth Haint turned, Dolittle found himself in the fog of suffocating darkness again.

"Blasted!" Dolittle shouted. "Haint! Where'd you go?"

Arms extended, he groped as he timidly shuffled forward, like a blind man. Again, he felt a sense of gravity and lunged, at once feeling the haint's hooded garment brush against his face. Catching two fistfuls of fabric in his hands, he worked his way around the haint's form until the world and faint traces of light re-appeared.

The stars barely twinkled, being outshone by the brightness of the full moon. As Dolittle glanced around, he realized he stood next to the haint in a seedy area of town—the red-light district.

On one corner, he saw a tall black teenager, hands in and out his coat pocket as he passed drugs to a white businessman. Farther down the street, he could see a group of men stealing the tires off a Lincoln Towncar. Several well-dressed young women and young men stood outside the lobby of a hotel, displaying negotiable fleshly pleasures for guests from around the world.

Still clutching the Fourth Haint's garment, Dolittle turned with the haint down a dark, unlit street, walking slowly along until Dolittle tripped over something and fell to the ground. When he looked back, he saw the faint, indistinct traces of a woman's body sprawled on the ground. Thinking her incapacitated or dead, he stood, looking down on the body.

She was wearing very little for such a cold night. Her red dress was short—upper thigh, and she wore no stockings and stiletto high heel shoes. The mop of blond hair on her head was obviously a wig, and her thick make-up disguised what appeared to be a pretty face. Her legs were shapely, with round hips, a narrow waist and an ample bosom, *décolletage* pushed and presented provocatively beyond the fabric of the tight dress.

Dolittle knelt for a better look, extending his hand to touch her face, which was still warm. *At least she's alive!* he thought. Examining more closely, he noticed the bruising on her face and arms, a busted lip and a dried stream of blood trailing down to her chin. The woman had apparently been abused! He placed his hand on her shoulder, shaking gently.

"Miss, are you okay?" Dolittle asked.

Responding to his touch, her body jerked violently, and her eyes popped open. When she looked upon Dolittle's face, a sense of terror flooded her expression and she let out an ear-piercing scream that seemed to reverberate in his head for a full minute afterward.

"It's you!" she said and screeched again.

"No, no!" Dolittle pleaded. "I found you lying here. I'm only trying to help you!"

"No! You're *one* of them!" she insisted while recoiling and trying to cover her exposed flesh.

"I'm trying to help you," Dolittle said softly, while removing his outer garment. "You're cold. Here—take my *robe*."

He realized the problem with the optics all too late—the vision of a man, standing over a scantily-clad, abused female victim, taking off his robe—not good! She had barely begun to scream again when he heard the loud voice.

"Step away from the woman! Now! And show me your hands!"

Dolittle looked over to see a police officer, gun drawn and aimed at his naked chest. Scanning over, a second officer also had his weapon drawn and trained at center mass.

"Get down on your knees, boy! Now!"

Again? Dolittle thought. *Now I understand the protests! How could anyone endure this non-stop persecution?*

The officer waved a hand twice before the woman's face to confirm his suspicion.

"Are you blind, ma'am?"

"Yes. He and his friends did this to me!" the woman wept, pointing in the direction of the half-naked man. "They've been abusing me! Pimping me out! They've forced me into a life of prostitution!"

"She's *lying*, Officer!" Dolittle screamed as the second policeman forced him onto his stomach, angrily twisting his arms back and clicking on the handcuffs. "I don't even *know* that woman! I've never seen her before! I just found her lying unconscious there!"

"No! *He's* lying!" she insisted. "He did see me earlier. We talked. We have a history! He gave me his card earlier tonight and told me to call him. I have it right here!"

The first officer took and read the card.

"Are you Thomas Dolittle, sir?" he asked. "It says here you're a *judge*?"

"No!" Dolittle said, frustrated. "I mean yes. I am a judge, but I have no history with her."

"Then what was this blind woman doing with your card?" the second officer asked. "And why were you standing over her body with your clothes half off? Did you do this to her? This poor vulnerable woman?"

"Hell no!" Dolittle retorted. "I've had enough of this mistreatment by you cops. I pay your salary! How *dare* you insinuate—"

Yet before Dolittle could finish the words, the first cop pushed him, knocking him to the ground, where his head slammed hard against the concrete. The impact caused his skin to split open, with profuse bleeding.

Rising to an elbow, he looked up in disbelief at the officer who shoved him. Ignoring the wound, the man set upon the judge, forcing him onto his stomach before twisting his arms harshly and tightening the cuffs.

"It's easy to abuse a poor blind woman when you're bigger than she is," the man said. "The tables turn when it's someone your own size. You're goin to jail, loser!"

Blood trailing down his face, Dolittle looked toward the Fourth Haint, who still stood there, watching silently. When it turned away, the utter darkness returned, but when the haint turned again toward Dolittle, the judge found himself in a bright courtroom at a table, wearing the orange jumpsuit of an accused felon. A public defender, who literally seemed more weasel than man, sat next to him.

At the other table sat the woman who had accused him, along with an elite team of lawyers, men and women of different races and backgrounds, who glanced over at him in derision and pre-judgment. The accuser was scarcely recognizable *sans* the wig and heavy make-up, while she was wearing a well-crafted flowing conservative wrap.

The prosecutor was a well-dressed, good-looking black woman with political ties who was known for her laser-focused interrogation tactics and progressive values. She stood, shaking her head as she cast condemning eyes upon Dolittle prior to her opening statement.

"This is a case about a man who has been harassing, threatening, abusing and doing his damnedest to control my client, Justice Themis," the prosecutor said, "after she vehemently refused to relinquish her independence to him and his powerful friends and associates. Ms. Themis has always cherished her independence, but against her will, this Judge Dolittle and his friends have forced her into a life of prostitution and shame. They have sold her body to rich and powerful interests. They have stolen her virtue. Judge Dolittle used his position of power to take advantage of her.

"That is why we are here today, ladies and gentlemen of the jury. My name is Destiny Mitchell, and I represent Ms. Themis, who is legally blind. In this trial, we ask you to restore her independence and punish this deplorable, unprincipled man and his colleagues for the unprecedented moral and ethical crimes they have committed against her."

"That's malarkey!" Dolittle whispered to the public defender. "I have done nothing of the sort, Mr. Lyndsey. She's lying. This is slander. Stand and defend me!"

Then the mealy-mouth public defender stood, stuttering, mumbling as he began.

"Your Honor," he said. "Ladies and gentlemen of the jury: you must dismiss this unsubstantiated case, because my client has done absolutely nothing wrong... or at least nothing *illegal*—end of story. There is no law granting Ms. Themis any natural right to independence. She *worked* for my client, and in his employ, he had the right to define or redefine her duty and responsibility as he and colleagues saw fit.

"My client has suffered injury and embarrassment as a result of this baseless accusation, and we demand an immediate end to this public spectacle. Because nothing can or will ever be *proven* by the other side in this matter, the entire exercise is nothing more than a smear on my client's good reputation."

When Dolittle looked up, he found himself seated on the witness stand on a dais, with the cosmopolitan prosecutor standing over him, her face expressing contempt.

"Ms. Themis also contends that you never paid her what she was owed, Judge Dolittle. What did you owe her?"

"Personally," he said, "I owed her nothing. Paying her was not my responsibility, though it was my understanding she was paid."

"Ms. Themis had been violently beaten and raped minutes before the authorities came upon you standing over her while taking off your clothes," the prosecutor continued. "Did you also rape her, Judge?"

"No!" Dolittle snapped back angrily, offended by the lurid suggestion.

"Did your friends and associates rape and otherwise abuse her, Judge?" she asked.

"I can't speak for other people I know and what they've done," Dolittle answered. "You're accusing me of doing something I would never do."

"Did you know she was being raped over the course of years?" Destiny asked. "Better yet, did you know she had been forced by powerful men to submit her body and virtue to other powerful men to satisfy their personal desires and political ends?"

"Not until she made that allegation when she asked for my help last night," Dolittle answered.

"So why didn't you help her, Dolittle?" the prosecutor asked.

"I told her I would do something if I had proof," he responded. "I found her claim implausible."

"And when you saw her later in the night, demoralized, beaten-up and raped, did you find her injuries plausible then?"

"Of course I did," he answered. "I saw them with my own eyes."

"So what did you do?" she asked.

"I tried to help her," he insisted.

"How?"

"I offered her my robe," he answered.

"A cover-up? And you thought *that* was helping her?" she continued, disgusted. "A woman tells you she's being abused and raped and begs you to help her, and you offer her a robe. How is *that* helping her?"

"I, I was showing her compassion," he answered.

"Showing compassion is not the same thing as helping," the prosecutor, stated. "This woman needed your help, and you failed her, and because you refused to help, she was raped repeatedly and beaten to near death. And you think you don't bear any responsibility for what happened because you heard her case and did nothing?"

"No."

"You had a duty to justice, Dolittle, and you did nothing," the lawyer asserted. "You offered her a cover-up? But did you seek to find out *who* was assaulting her, even if that meant investigating and prosecuting the behavior of some of your closest friends and associates?"

"I guess not," he answered.

"And once you saw her there, abused and raped," Destiny continued, "did you call for those found guilty of these heinous crimes against her to be punished to the fullest extent of the law?"

"No. Once again, I'm being falsely blamed," Dolittle fumed. "It's the system—not me! Your romantic view of justice is unrealistic. It's not how things work in the actual court."

The prosecutor sighed, again wagging her head.

"And that, Judge Dolittle, makes you complicit. *Some men wish evil and accomplish it,* in the words of writer Steven Benet, *but most men, when they work in the machine, just let it happen somewhere in the wheels.* You stood by and let it happen. You allowed the abuse and rape to continue."

"It wasn't my place!" Dolittle insisted.

Hearing that comment, Justice lost her temper and bolted up from her seat. "Liar," she screamed. "Don't pretend you don't know what happens to me behind closed doors!"

"Dr. King said it best," Destiny continued. *"He who passively accepts evil is as much involved in it as he who helps to perpetrate it. He who accepts evil without protesting against it is really cooperating with it.*"

"I tell you it was not my business," Dolittle insisted.

"Justice is the most important business of a judge," Destiny asserted.

"I've heard enough," concluded Judge Sullivan, who spoke from a lofty bench of judicial thought. "Thomas Dolittle, an empirical jury of the people has found you guilty of the crime of aiding and abetting in the dishonor and ruination of Miss Justice Themis. Thus you are hereby sentenced to your very *own* dishonor and ruination in perpetuity throughout recorded history."

"I object to your ruling!" Dolittle shouted in his defense. "May I make a statement, Your Honor?"

"You already have, Dolittle," the admirable judge countered. "Your *life* and your decisions are your statement, for now and ever more."

When the scene went dark, Dolittle realized that the Third Haint had turned toward the next lesson, or revelation, and yet, though Dolittle pivoted in all eight directions, he remained consumed in darkness. As he stumbled and groped in no path, there was a flash of a scene in a strobe light effect, a scene in which he saw himself wrapped in smaller links, graduating to the huge, heavy, intransigent links of a monstrous chain. He saw himself struggling futilely to escape that torture while he was forced to live out nonstop the last few moments of black lives lost in real time.

Marshall tried to help me, he thought. *Perhaps it was that selfless act, the demonstration and fulfillment of his duty to justice that brought escape from his tortures...*

"Third Haint!" called Dolittle out into the tarry nighttime abyss, "please pity me yet and save me! Help me to avoid this ascribed bitter judgement yet-to-come!"

In an instant, Dolittle found himself standing again on a crowded street in the Chocolate City, on a freezing cold sunny day with the darkest haint on his right side, his aspect turned toward a small group of black women, who instantly stopped and gawked upon seeing Dolittle.

"They can *see* me?" Dolittle asked. "I thought we were shadows! They obviously can't see you."

Slowly, he recognized where he was—somewhere off U Street in the corridor known as Black Broadway. Duke Ellington had grown up in a house down the street.

"That's him!" one of the women called out. "I'd know that face anywhere! Jive turkey."

The other women approached cautiously, glancing side-eye, though growing bolder.

"That *is* him!" another woman said. "I thought he got convicted and condemned. *Thank ya, Jesus!* What's he doing out here? He's dangerous!"

"Someone call the police," a third woman warned. "He musta escaped from prison."

"He got more to worry about than the police in *this* neighborhood," the first woman argued. "Nobody trusts him down here. Let folks in the neighborhood find out he's here. Maybe *then* he'll find out what a real lynchin is. Let's follow him!"

"Haint!" the judge complained. "They can *see* me! They're following me."

Dolittle thought he could make an escape behind the haint, but no matter how hard he tried to conceal himself in the haint's darkness, the haint would reposition to expose him in the light, with the growing group of women still in pursuit.

While struggling to keep a distance, he stumbled into a pick-up game of basketball in a park, where two games were being played simultaneously. There were twenty black teens and young adults on the court, with another twenty at courtside waiting to play the winners.

As he glanced back at the women, Dolittle accidentally crashed into a teenage boy as the baller drove for the basket. His unwitting pick had knocked the youth to the ground.

"I'm very sorry, young man," Dolittle stuttered. "My fault. I wasn't paying attention to where I was going."

"Man," the youth responded. "I ain't nevva been checked so hard in my life! What are you doin here? Waitaminute!"

Dolittle bowed his head and tried to move beyond the game.

"Hold on!" the tall youth said to his teammates. "Is that who I *think* that is? Fellas—isn't that Thomas Dolittle, the black judge?"

"You're right. That's him," one of the women answered. "He ain't never done right by us. That's why we ain't lettin him get away."

By that time, Dolittle was hurrying off the court.

"Where's he goin?" the youth asked.

"I don't think even he knows that," the woman responded, "but we gonna follow behind him until he has some answers for us."

Although Dolittle had increased his pace, when he looked back over his shoulder, he realized the crowd pursuing him had increased three-fold. A huge portion from the basketball court were also close behind.

"Oh no!" he said as he looked ahead. "Good Lord!"

Directly before him was a large group, composed of African American families, just beginning to march in some organized demonstration—men, women and children, carrying placards and engaged in the call and response of black protest. Notwithstanding, it wasn't long before they discovered who he was and re-committed the hundreds assembled to pursue and task the nervous judge. Yet the more Dolittle hurried, the closer the great crowd bore down upon him.

When he realized he would never outrun his tormenters, he decided it would be best if he steeled himself enough to turn around to face them. He closed his eyes, remembering his grandfather, and then he stopped, before turning. Only to his surprise, when he turned around, he was not alone. His nephew, Freddie, stood boldly beside him.

"What do you all want with my uncle?" Freddie demanded.

"Accountability," a protester from the church demanded. "The judge has done nothing to help black people. He's done the opposite—he's taken sides against anything that would help the black community."

"Why do you hate black people?" an eight-year-old girl in the crowd called out.

"Why *would* I hate black people?" Dolittle asked. "I've been black all my life."

"You've accounted for more blacks dyin than the KKK," a light-skinned woman said. "Your legacy as a black man gave you the power of a great judge to help, when all you do is hurt us, devalue our lives and dishonor us. Answer that, Dolittle!"

"What have you ever done to *help* us?" Nat, an activist asked.

"When was it ever my *responsibility* to specifically help you?" Dolittle countered.

"When you took over for *Marshall*, that's when!" Nat shouted back angrily. "Your job was to continue his stewardship, and you've done nothing for it so far. You left off it!"

"Marshall had his priorities, and I have mine!" Dolittle answered. "They don't have to be the same priorities."

"Marshall had his legacy, which he owed to those who came before him," Nat answered. "That's the legacy that you inherited and owe, like it or not. Any power you have comes from it. It's the *same* legacy, you old fool!"

When the crowd pressed closer, the judge held out a hand in protest.

"You ignorant people—I knew you wouldn't listen," Dolittle said, "but I am not about to put up with threats and condemnation from the likes of you. If you come any closer, I'll call the police!"

His warning had the opposite effect. Several strong sturdy men from the crowd immediately laid hands on Dolittle, lifting him helpless, high into the air.

"We have no use for you," the activist man said. "None of ours is better than *one* of ours who is blind and cannot see himself, or us. Even the judge will not escape judgment. He ain't nothin but his granddaddy—Hannibal Thomas—come back! This Judas gotta pay taday, blood fa blood!"

"Wait!" Dolittle's nephew, Freddie, called to the crowd while placing a hand on his uncle's head. "You cannot condemn him, nor can you ignore his right to his own independence. I completely disagree with his beliefs and attitudes, but I must argue that even he represents the freedom of independent thought in our community."

"Not him!" a woman contended. "If he didn't want the weight of the black community on his shoulders, then he nevva shoulda took the job as our judge. He owes us."

"I'm not your judge. I owe you nothing!" Dolittle shot back, defiant.

"No Justice, No Peace!" the massive dark crowd shouted, "This Justice, Must Cease!"

"Ma Daddy always told me!" Nat said, "I brought you inta this world, and I can take you out. We are the *reason* you're a judge, Dolittle, and now we're takin you out, by any means necessary. You're now on our shoulders. It's judgment time, traitor!"

Nephew Freddie took a place between his uncle and his impending consequences. "No!" he pleaded. "There *is* good in my uncle. I see it even if he doesn't! If you are bent on action, take me in his place, but let him go. Allow him his independence so he can find his way home in time."

"He's committed crimes against the black community," Nat insisted. "He's blood-guilty. There must be justice."

"Then let *me* pay his debt," Freddie said, "so that he may see himself through my sacrifice."

"You understand the consequences?" Nat asked.

"I'm ready," Freddie said. "I'll proudly die to save your soul, Uncle."

Upon a nod from Nat, the men put Dolittle down and instead laid hands on Freddie, taking him up. Still shaking, the fearful, grateful judge looked up into the eyes of his damned nephew.

"Freddie, why are you doing this?"

"You're family, and in this world, that *has* to mean something. But more important, it is the right thing to do."

"I cannot let you do this," the judge asserted.

"It's already done," Freddie said, weeping. "One ask, Uncle—one request of you! I beg you: please go to my wife, Harri, and to my children—please tell them I loved them and beg from them forgiveness for my sacrifice."

In that instant, Freddie's flesh turned dark and fell as powder to the ground, leaving behind the bleached bones of a skeleton in place of his form. Yet Dolittle had little time to grieve before he found himself before the door to a modest home in the bowels of the city.

"I know who you are!" Harri said after she opened the door. "You're Uncle Tom—no, I mean, Uncle Thomas. Freddie's told me all about you!"

"My nephew and I never saw things eye-to-eye. You must think I'm horrible."

"No!" Harri exclaimed. "No, not at all. Freddie *loves* you. He respects you. He's always said you're gonna make us all so proud."

"Really?"

"He's never lost faith in you, even when so many others have," she said, "even though you lost your way. For years, he's been tellin me and the kids that you're coming for Black Sunday Dinner, and even when you haven't, he's always set a place at the table for you."

"Black Sunday Dinner?"

"Oughta be an unofficial national holiday," Harri answered. "Since the King holiday is always celebrated on a Monday, black families across the country now take that Sunday night to come together to celebrate family as they contemplate history—past, present and what will come. You just never showed up. Why now?"

"Freddie's dead."

"What? Come again?"

"That's what I said," Dolittle answered, "and he wanted me to tell you and the kids he loved you and he was sorry."

"No! Not my Freddie! How?" she asked, beginning to weep. "What happened?"

Dolittle hung his head, and he felt especially remorseful when his nephew's children, Miles, a teenaged son, and Kamala, a 13-year-old, came into the room, first to comfort their mother and then to succumb to their own grief, shrieking and wailing and begging to know "why?"

"It was for me," Dolittle answered, thinking. "He sacrificed himself for me... I think he did it so I could finally be here with you—so that I would finally see you, and him *through* you."

Still reacting to the news of his father's death, Miles collapsed to the floor, clutching his legs.

"Oh no! Miles," Harri sighed, "you're having a pain crisis. Just be still and breathe, like we practiced!"

"A pain crisis?" Dolittle asked.

"He has sickle cell anemia, Uncle," Harri answered. "The stress of your news about his father has caused an episode. Kamala—call Dr. McCune Smith! Tell im we're on our way to the hospital."

"I'm sorry, Harri," Dolittle groaned as he glanced at the teenager, struggling on the floor. "I'm sorry that I never took the time to see you and know you."

"Uncle," she said, "I can't help but remember the last conversation Freddie and I had. It was about the difference between thinkers and doers. He was always a thinker, but as a doer, I've become a thinker—enough to realize that, in the end, Freddie became a doer. You can be a doer as well."

It was obvious that the Third Haint had turned to the next lesson when the darkness suddenly returned, but then, in spite of the darkness, a bright light shined around Dolittle from heaven and an unseen blunt force knocked him to the ground, and then a voice.

"Thomas," the voice said, "why are you persecuting me?"

"Persecuting you?" Dolittle asked. "Who are you?"

"I am the one you are persecuting," the voice answered.

Terrified, Dolittle asked, "I think I understand, but what would you have me do?"

"You already know," the voice answered. "You can no longer avoid it. You must face the inevitability of your destiny. You must resume the true path you once began, the one you abandoned in your misconstruction. You, alone and at last, must answer to your legacy."

When Dolittle rose to his feet, he found himself standing on the porch of a white cinderblock house, the ceiling of which was painted a distinctive pale blue-green. The Third Haint, standing next to him, seemed smaller and less imposing, and its feet in worn work shoes were planted on the wooden deck. As it turned toward the judge, the hooded garment fell off, revealing the likeness of an old black man who Dolittle most definitely recognized.

Dolittle stood there transfixed, heart pounding, hardly able to breathe. In the many years that had passed since he got the sad though expected news, he had never imagined he would look into those stern eyes again.

The silent Third Haint had taken on the likeness of his grandfather to speak the unspoken words that Dolittle feared for years hearing his candid grandfather speak. Dolittle had been haunted for decades by the silent condemnation, imprinted on his heart and whispered inside his head in the bass Gullah voice of his lost grandfather.

I ain't gotta say a word, boy," he said. "Ya already know what's in my head. I told you first day you come ta nevva shame me, or ta nevva shame yo race. You thought I was gone, but I been right here, watchin everythang. You've heard me talkin ta ya, but you ain't been listenin."

"Daddy!" Dolittle said, "You were gone. I *thought* I heard you sometimes, but I've had to make my own decisions, I've had to live my life as I've seen fit."

"I ain't nevva been gone," the old man insisted, "I been right here. I'm alive as long as you alive! Until no day is clean, until there is no mornin, no sunrise."

"But you're dead," Dolittle insisted.

"And you dead, boy," the Third Haint snapped. "You just don't know it yet. We all dead before long! I just cain't do nothin about my place now, but you still can."

"Daddy," Dolittle admitted sadly, "I need to say this: I'm sorry I allowed distance to grow between us before you died. I thought for sure we would come together and make things better. I was convinced we'd have that last good talk."

"Life ain't long enough for 'sorry'," the old man answered. "It's done been time for that talk. Tell me, boy, what have you done with your life?"

"I've tried to be the best person I could be," Dolittle answered. "I've tried to live up to the standards that you instilled in me. I tried to make you proud."

The silence of the Third Haint had returned. Dolittle sensed it, though he continued anyway.

"From the time I was a boy, I always worked hard at any task before me, whether it was workin on a fence at the farm or studying for my classes. I knew all honest work was good work. I held high expectations for myself."

Dolittle looked for a reaction from the old man, but he received none.

"None of us can control the time, place and circumstances into which we are born. I was born poor and black, to an unwed mother, at a time when being black was a life sentence to inferiority and racial persecution, and in a country where it was essentially criminal to be black.

"Whether it was good fortune or the will of God, I was given an opportunity to transcend my circumstances, provided that I was willing to stubbornly adhere to the principles of hard work and honesty.

"My dedicated grandfather instilled a sense of justice in me, which remains today. For that reason, it made me angry that the vast majority of my black brothers and sisters in this country were living an inferior American Dream, forced to accept second-class citizenship, and worse, we were forced to offer ourselves as living sacrifices in order to merely exist in America.

"Our ancestors, our fathers and mothers, sisters and brothers, children and kin—tens of thousands were dead each year, in lynchings, hate crimes, medical and legal indifference and malpractice on every level, economic inequality, false imprisonment and the destruction of our dreams and self-worth.

"When I was in college, I experienced prejudice and discrimination on the institutional level, so I got involved as an activist. I marched with the Black Panthers and called for the freeing of Angela Davis. I was secretary of the Black Student Union, and I supported multiple left-wing causes. Yet through the actual experience, I came to an epiphany. I eventually understood that a liberal mentality only made circumstances *worse* for black people. It only made them more dependent on whites, less self-reliant and less inclined to believe and work hard for better outcomes.

"As a black realist, I became a conservative, and my political positions have placed me at odds with the majority of African Americans, who remain liberal, though they can't tell anyone why or what liberals have actually done for them over the last ninety years.

"Notwithstanding, they hate me and call me traitor and *Uncle Tom*, but my life and my choices have been the result of the lessons and principles that *you* instilled in me, Daddy. I understand that now. I only wish I could have appreciated your wisdom more when I had the chance."

"I'm sure all that makes *you* feel better, boy," the Third Haint slowly responded, "but it makes me know that all I did was raise an *educated fool*! Ya calls yoself a conservative, an that's all good, but it don't make ya smarter or better'n nobody else, black or *buckra*. I ain't educated, but even I know conservative is what you *think an believe*, not who you are. Ya long been forgot who you are an where you come from."

"I haven't forgotten!" Dolittle fumed. "I'm a Supreme Court Justice. That could have never happened if I had gone back there, back home!"

"Ah tol ja the day ya decided ta go up North," the haint sighed. "I said ya was gonna end up juss like yo father and the other no-good Negroes at home. I hate ta say it I was right."

"How can you say that about me, Daddy?" Dolittle asked, his feelings bruised. "My father ran out on us. He took and felt no obligation to look out after us. For whatever his reasons, he failed to live up to his responsibility for his family. He did nothing."

"Ain't that what you done, boy?" his grandfather said, "when ya run out on us back at home? When ya turnt ya back on yo family? Ya turnt you back on yo people, juss like yo father turnt his back on you. Some niggas—ya give em two suits and an attaché case, an they forget they folks. Remember Martin—he *stayed*, an that's why he's respected and remembered."

"I worked my butt off to become something!" Dolittle scoffed. "What do I owe black people?"

"Ya smellin yaself, boy! What did I owe *you* when I took ya in an tried to brang ya up ta make us proud, and ya *race* proud? the haint asked. "No one's proud of ya, no one but yaself."

"I think some people are proud of me…" Dolittle insisted.

"Why would them buckra be proud of ya?" the spirit returned. "You ain't nevva been, an you ain't nevva gone be no *buckra*, no matter how much ya wanna. Don't be no joke fa them *buckra*, boy! Don't let em make a foola ya life! They usin the color of ya black skin as a weapon against the rest of us, so buck *up*! I didn't raise ya ta be no blind main, or chupid!"

"That's not true," Dolittle protested, defensive.

"Ya got a lotta power as a judge," Daddy insisted. "You, who grew up a black boy in *ma* house. Name for me one thang ya done for black folks since they put you up there?"

"Excuse me, Daddy," Dolittle said, "but black people didn't put me up where I am. I *earned* my place."

"Naw," Daddy answered, "Claire fo God—*they* earned ya place, by they sweat, they sacrifice and they blood! Why you think you up there? Cuz you was the best judge in the country they could fine? Like it or not, you *up* there cuz you was black, an they needed a black ta take the *place* of a black. You owe black back somethin. And ya *know* you ain't done right by ya race."

"That's a racist thing to say, Daddy," Dolittle answered. "No judge should ever give preferences to black people, or white or green people for that matter. The rule of law should be colorblind."

"But yo damn rule of law ain't *no* kinda blind—it ain't nevva done right by black folks!" the old man answered. "I think sometimes, as a black man, ya gotta pull that blind down a little bit and peek out every once in a while, juss ta make sure the rest of em is doin right by us—ya peoples. You owe us at least that much. Come *home*, boy. Please come on home!"

In that moment, Dolittle reflected on the haints that had preceded this Third Haint. He reflected on the spirit of Marshall and his warning about an extra-judicial duty to justice. Then he thought of the First Haint and the history of injustice in America through racist and immoral laws, court rulings, good and bad, and a long history of struggle, the first fruits of which were unripe, meager and under-sized.

He thought of the Second Haint and America's never-ending, centuries-long litany of injustice, from coast to coast, from North to South. Imprinted in his psyche were the hundreds of unarmed black men, women and children dead each year at the hands of law enforcement, the millions incarcerated and the overwhelming, irrepressible spirit of the protests. He derived rare hope from the determination of the protesters, who at personal sacrifice and at great risk hailed from every race, age group and every other definable demographic.

Finally, he remembered the silence of the Third Haint, who allowed the spirit of Injustice-Yet-to Come to speak for itself. He shook his head at the realization of the identity of the persecuted woman who had come to him, pleading for aid and independence, before he had turned her away.

So in answer to the Third Haint, who had said, *You owe us at least that much*, Dolittle responded, "For you, I'll take the matter under advisement."

"Well, if a Catholic Cardinal can vow ta be a voice for the African American community, then a judge like you can at least listen better and appreciate 400 of years strugglin with injustice."

"I suppose I could," Dolittle shrugged.

"I don't got no law degree, but I has a life degree," Daddy said, nodding. "What do they call that in the law where somethin is passed down from one generation ta the next?"

"It's called an inheritance," Dolittle answered, "a legacy."

"Let it be that, then," the Third Haint concluded. "Please undastan: I'm not askin ya to go back on what ya believe in yo heart. I'm juss askin ya ta meet ya peoples halfway. Ya gotta recognize that what ya received really *was* an inheritance, but not your inheritance. It's been an will always be *ours*, not yours. You a steward with a great responsibility ta only make that inheritance betta before ya pass it on ta the next steward. If ya don't change, then when ya die, that legacy dies with ya!"

"I never saw it that way," Dolittle admitted.

"Then move out ya own way!" Daddy shouted. "You cain't see it cuz ya standin in the way of history. See the bigga day, from early mornin ta late night, ta a *betta* day. Come back *home*, boy. Ya shoulda nevva left us!"

After saying that, Daddy turned, and in his place stood the silent, frightening shrouded Third Haint, seeming even larger and more intimidating than before. When it moved forward, Dolittle followed to avoid being consumed by the gravity of the creeping and irresistible darkness in the creature's wake.

When the light returned, Dolittle found himself in a brightly-lit silent room, smelling of antiseptic. As he looked out the open door, he watched nurses rushing by, one way and then the other. He saw doctors in the corridor on occasion, so he realized he was in a hospital room. Rushing to the door, he called out questions to nurses who passed by, but none could see him and two passed directly through him! *Why was he in a hospital?*

Re-entering the room, he walked over to the single empty bed, where there was a chart attached to the footrail. After he took of the chart and began reading, he realized he was in the State of Maryland at Bethesda Hospital, or Walter Reed. The patient once occupying the bed was suffering from complications of a bad heart. But then he saw something that baffled his curiosity and brought an instant dread. It was the name on the chart: *Thomas C. Dolittle.*

Glancing up, he realized the bed was not empty at all, as he had initially thought. There was the shape of a body under the crisp white sheet. Against his own will, he took a step toward the top of the bed and pulled the sheet down, gasping as his mind struggled with the immediate shock of what he witnessed then. He saw himself, his own body, naked as a j-bird, eyes wide open, lying there dead!

"No, Haint!" Dolittle cried out. "This can't be! Surely this is just another lesson. Please tell me I'm not dead!"

The Third Haint stood beside him, unstirring, neither saying a word.

"I, I know you don't talk," Dolittle said, "but can you at least give me a sign, maybe a head nod? Is this real, or is it a shadow of something yet-to-come? Is there anything I can do to change this, to stop it from happening? The legacy can't die!"

Unmoving silence was the haint's answer.

"When Marshall came to see me, he said I could save myself. You have to give me a chance to change! Otherwise, what was the point of this night and all that I experienced? You have to answer me! Just give me a sign, please!"

Dolittle scarce believed his eyes when the creature moved, striking a pose, which was familiar, though he was unsure of its meaning. Bowing its head, its left arm pointed upward and extended, its right arm across its chest and also pointed upward, the creature appeared to do "the Dab."

"What is the significance of that gesture?" Dolittle begged. "Are you pointing me toward God? Does that mean I might have a chance to make things right? Oh, please save me, God! For from this moment on, I'll honor the legacy that I inherited from history and share with so many others! I promise I'll be a good steward to that legacy!

"I will always have conservative views—that is who I am, unapologetically, but I will *find* ways to honor my grandfather, my family, my race and all victims of injustice. I'll re-examine the history of injustice in America. I'll value the unsung, underappreciated heroes who fought and sacrificed their lives, quick and dead, for an inheritance, despite daunting, historically hopeless circumstances. And I'll carry with me my full history and background as a judge.

"As a judge, my primary duty is justice, but I have an equal if not more persistent duty to address *injustice* and injustices, which if even they occurred in the past, they affect injustice today and impact injustice yet-to-come. Oh, please hear my supplication. I have listened tonight and learned well by it: I am and will be the reluctant steward of a hard-fought and enduring legacy!"

He reached out, grasping hold of the Third Haint's arm, determined not to release it without the gift and promise of another opportunity, and even though the dark haint seemed to resist, Dolittle held on stubbornly. At last, the haint threw him aside, but Dolittle persisted there, hands clasped in prayerful entreaty.

And finally, after a tenuous contemplative pause, the haint seemed to relent and at once dissolved, abandoning the dark shroud that fell to the floor, transforming to a blanket. In the place where Dolittle had clutched one of the haint's bony arms was one of the smooth ebony posts from the bed's headboard.

SHOUT V

SHOUT V
And That's That

Yes! and the bedpost was his own.

"Thank you, Jesus!" Dolittle sighed as he looked about the room. It was that same feeling he had upon returning to a familiar place after a long journey. His desk, with an open laptop next to a stack of unopened mail, was a welcoming sight. The snifter next to the brandy decanter on the nightstand still contained a sip or two of the stale pale. His pillow, so close to his face, still smelled of the resin from the cedar-lined linen closet. *Ah! He was home!*

As he looked over at the digital clock, he realized that time had taken on an added relevance.

"From now on, I'll live in the Past, Present and Future," Dolittle pledged. "I'll recognize injustice when I see it, however disguised or rationalized!"

He rose from the bed, glancing toward a mirror, where he stood in his pajamas and nightcap, a humbled soul.

"As much as they frightened and tortured me, the haints of Injustice Past, Injustice Present and Injustice Yet-to-Come will remain with me as long as I'm alive," he said. "Oh Thoroughgood! Good friend and teacher, Thoroughgood! You have saved me from the Yet-to-Come. Thank God for you, my brother, in life and in death!"

As he changed into his day clothes, he looked at the floor, the window and the curtains, which in recent memory he saw engulfed in flames, radiating infernal heat, consumed in a hellish conflagration.

Chastened, he fell to his knees, where he sobbed violently, his conservative ideology at conflict with all three Spirits of Injustice, yet in his own humbled spirit there began a growing reconciliation, a resolution and a new synthesis.

Standing at his desk, he looked down on the statue of Janus, a physical reminder of his intellectual transition.

"Whether dream or vision," he said, "I have been visited by three haints who spoke and revealed truths beyond my reckoning. Yet the sun and sanity have returned. My room destroyed is again as it was, the bedsheets, curtains, and walls unsinged.

"I saw the shadows of Injustice Past, Injustice Present, and even the shadow of Injustice Yet-to-Come, and while I cannot change the former two, I will strive with all my being to change the latter."

Hearing the church bells clanging in the distance, he went to the window and threw the panels open, welcoming the grey light of the morning, fluorescent beneath bright featureless clouds. The sun shone through an opening in the distance, a slanted golden ray that illuminated the courthouse.

"What day is it today?" Dolittle called out to a little black boy and black girl who seemed to be dressed for church.

The children hesitated, remembering their grandfather told them that the judge had slipped one day and fell in a way that he had sat directly on a stick... *and it was still there!*

"It's Sunday," the older bolder girl answered, "but not just any Sunday. Tomorrow's the King holiday, so today's Black Sunday Dinner. We celebratin that today."

"We gonna be grubbin tanite!" the boy said, grinning.

"It's more than that," she interrupted, embarrassed. "It's about families celebrating having each other and what we been through together."

"And what our ancestors been through," the boy added.

"Yeah," she nodded, "that too. It's a day of remembrance before we pause to recognize the legacy that brought us Dr. King and the legacy that he left for us."

"Then I haven't missed either?" Dolittle asked.

"Either *what*?" she remarked.

"The dinner and the holiday!" Dolittle exclaimed. "I've never recognized either, but this year I'll celebrate both!"

And That's That

As a humbled man, Dolittle looked closer, and finally he saw the children, their eyes and their expressions.

"I'm sorry," he said. "I know you're my neighbors, but I don't even know your names. I'm... I'm, uh, Thomas..."

"Ma name's Ernestine," the girl said, "an this is ma brotha, Frank."

"You a strange man, sir," Frank said. "Did ja *really* fall and sit on a stick though?"

His sister, channeling their mother, gave him the stank-eye and instantly popped him upside his head.

Excited about the prospect of celebrating the day, Dolittle hardly heard the question, asking his own instead.

"Georgia Brown's on 15th? Is that place still open for take-out?" he asked.

"Yes, sir," the girl answered, "but it's Black Family Dinner. They probably done run outta food."

"We'll see about *that!*" Dolittle said as he grabbed his overcoat and threw it over his shoulders. "Thank you, children. I'd like to walk with you to church if you let me, but I won't be able to stay long. There are a few things I have to do, things I have to make right."

"No, thank you," the boy piped out. "We don't walk with strangers."

"That's Judge Dolittle, boy," the girl whispered between her teeth. "Mama been prayin bout him for years! Cain't hurt for him ta see inside of a Black Church."

Dolittle hurried downstairs, and as he walked with the children, he asked about their family, their ambitions and their struggles.

"I'm sorry, Mista Dolittle," the girl explained, "but it's mostly people like you, who be sittin up there, watchin people die. Don't cha see it on the news? Y'all pretend ta be *good* people who care about us, but ya don't. Ma granmamma say the proof is always in the puddin. Sayin ain't the same as doin."

Dolittle took a seat in the back of the church, full of black families. He bowed his head, hoping he wouldn't be recognized, and he sat listening as the sermon began.

"Who is my neighbor?" the young preacher began. "Who *really* is my neighbor? Well, as we spend this weekend contemplating the life and example of Dr. King, I'm going to tell you a story you've probably heard before in one way or another. It's the sad story of a man who suffers a great injustice. He's walking down the street, mindin his business, when he's attacked by a group of... well, let's call em thugs. Anyway, they rob him, beat him savagely and leave him for dead, sufferin a great injustice. So he was just kinda lyin there, bloody, broken, sayin *Why me?* when he saw someone comin his way.

"The guy he saw was sportin a color—blue, which the sufferin man immediately recognized. Naw, he wasn't a 'Crip.' The blue he wore identified him as a 'liberal.' So the bloodied-up man said to himself, *Surely this man will help me, since liberals are known for their sympathy and advocacy toward the poor, disadvantaged and sufferin!*

"However, the liberal, when from a distance he set eyes upon the wounded man, he stopped, but not without lookin around to see if anyone was watchin im. You see, he was alone—in that place where true character reveals itself. So the liberal said to himself, *How can I be sure of what I saw? I have other things to do today. Maybe he was just takin a nap—better not wake him. He'll be alright.* And the liberal crossed the street and passed by on the other side.

"Then the wounded man saw another person comin, all dressed in red. No, he wasn't a 'Blood'—he was a 'conservative,' and the man said to himself, *Surely this man will help me, since conservatives are known for law and order, and are protectors of life, which they consider sacred, when surely I'm dyin here!*

"But the conservative, upon seein him, stopped in his tracks, wary, and so he said to himself, *How do I know this man is really a victim? Maybe it's a scheme to get over on me. Besides, I believe we are the authors of our own consequences. He is in that place as a result of his own misjudgment or error.* So the conservative crossed the street and passed by on the other side.

"But then a Good Citizen came along, an honest person of good values in ordinary clothes, and when he saw this man, beaten and suffering, he mourned and sighed with compassion. He immediately stopped, knelt, and without qualifying or judging, he worked to bind the beaten man's wounds.

"He got his car and drove the man over to a clinic for additional care, and then he took him to a hotel and rented a room where the injured man could recover. He paid the room for the next few days and left his credit card open in case there were additional expenses.

"It should be obvious," the young preacher said, "but I'll ask anyway: Which of these three men passing by was the true neighbor, or friend, of this man who suffered injustice?"

After a mélange of responses from the congregation, the preacher called on Ernestine to answer.

"The Good Citizen was the true neighbor," she shouted out in the huge church, "the one who showed him compassion and mercy."

"Amen! You're right, young sista!" the preacher said, "and if we're not already there, it's the place where we should begin!

*The Good Citizens, my brothas and sistas,
Are wearing neither red nor blue,
And we will recognize them, not
By what they say, but what they do."*

Dolittle rose immediately and headed for the door, determined to correct a recent error. He could have called an Uber or Lyft for a ride, but he decided to walk so he could rethink his convictions, sort out which among them came from his heart, and which ones were invasive, dogmatic and indoctrinated. And so he walked, block after block until he reached the glass and concrete building.

He stopped at a reception desk inside where two sheriff officers sat, engaged in a quiet conversation.

"I'm here to secure the release of three—no, I'm here to secure the release of *four* prisoners."

"I'm afraid that's not possible," the first officer said. "It's Sunday morning. We have no release order, none of the courts are open, and it would be impossible to get a judge to sign an order *this* morning of all mornings."

"I *am* a judge," Dolittle said, "and what's more, I am the citizen who signed the complaint against three of the four. I've had a change of heart."

Thirty minutes later, Dolittle stood outside the jailhouse with Martin, Malcolm, John and a grateful fourth young man.

"I've ordered rides for all of you, to wherever you need to go," Dolittle said.

"But I don't understand!" the fourth young man said. "I don't get it. Why are you doing this… for *me*?"

"Listen to your friends," Dolittle sighed, reflecting. "They understand."

"Well, I'm going to a march this mornin," John said. "Judge, I'd be obliged if you came along with me."

"Change takes time, maybe even a lifetime," Dolittle answered. "Besides, I have something else to do this morning."

Dolittle walked along, hoping the group would be assembled in that same spot, at that same intersection, *Protest* at *Acquiescence*. As he marched along, the clouds above began to dissipate, and the sun appeared in a bright blue sky. Only then did he see the people. He saw work clothes and worn shoes, he saw calloused hands and stooped backs, he saw trouble in worried faces and the last glints of hope in dimming, fading eyes.

Finally, he reached the group and sought out Will and Esperanza, asking here and there until he found them.

"You, Judge!" Will exclaimed. "Someone told me you had a heart attack."

"I guess news travels fast in the hood," Dolittle laughed. "I said I had a *change* of heart. It was the guard at the jail who almost had a heart attack."

"It's good to see you on this side, Judge," Esperanza smiled, "but why are you here?"

"I came to apologize for dismissing your case yesterday afternoon without giving it my earnest consideration..." the judge answered, "and I came to give you this."

He discreetly slipped her a check, though her response was less than restrained.

"Ten thousand dollars!" she gasped, "Are you *serious*?"

"It's been long overdue," the judge returned quietly. "From now on, you can count on my support in your struggle against injustice and its effects on our community."

"*Mah* nigga!" Will chortled as he smacked the judge on the back. "When I finally realized who you were, I thought you'd *nevva* come around."

"*Social distancing*!" the judge warned. "Well, here I am."

"Okay, but can you stick *around*?" Esperanza asked. "We really could use your voice in our movement and protest."

"Not for me," the judge answered, "but I will definitely be paying more attention."

"But can't you stick around for a bit?" Will persisted.

"I'm sorry," the judge answered, "but there are other things I have to do today."

As he hurried to his next destination, he literally bumped into Heschel, his skinny law clerk.

"I take it *this* is why you wanted the day off, Abe," the judge nodded, "to participate in the protest?"

"Yes," the clerk answered. "It may not seem like much, but every person and every voice make a difference... even when it seems hopeless."

"I think you're right," Dolittle said. "Today, your hope is rewarded. I've never told you how much I appreciate your hard work and dedication to principles of justice, so I'm firing you as my law clerk. When you come back on Tuesday, it will be as my personal assistant, my counterbalance, or living conscience, for twice the salary and better benefits!"

"Thank you, sir—I mean Judge, sir!" Heschel exclaimed as he stood in a near salute. "But I heard you were dead—that you had a heart attack."

"*Rumors of my demise have been greatly exaggerated*," Dolittle smirked with a smile. "With God, all things are possible. I'll see you on Tuesday."

He steeled himself as he continued walking toward his next destination on 23rd, the University Hospital. He didn't know why he knew, but he knew she would be there, and so when he got to the desk on the ground floor, he nodded toward the receptionist.

"I'm here to see a patient, a Miss Justice Themis?"

"Ah, you mean the blind woman, Jussie Law. Yes, she's here," the receptionist answered. "Are you an immediate family member or relative?"

"Yes," he said. "We've been estranged, but yes, I am a close relative."

He considered her blindness as he quietly approached the bed and took a seat next to her.

"Tho *now* you sthrow up, *coward man?*" she scoffed, speaking from the corner of her lips from a half-paralyzed face, "after you did nothing and let thisth happen to me!"

He was taken aback by the extent of her injuries. Her once pretty face was discolored, bruised and swollen, especially along the jawline. One of her pale, useless eyes was bloodshot, while the other was leaking pus and nearly sealed shut, crusted over. She had a bloodied bandage wrapped around her head, which was held upright by a metal brace, and her right arm was in traction. Her body showed signs of

And That's That

some cruel ravaging and torture. Her lower left leg was in a cast.

"I'm sorry," Dolittle said. "I should have trusted you. I should have believed you."

"I begged you, but you wouldn't *listhen*!" she hissed, a tear trailing from the open eye.

"I know, I know," he sadly admitted, "and I take full responsibility for what happened to you. I promise to make it up to you."

"Listhen, Thomasth," she said, straining to sit up. "You can't take full resthponsthibility, becausth it wasth'n justh you..."

Groaning, she took the saliva-dripping clear retainer from her mouth with bruised fingers, one nail bloody and missing.

"You men have been abusing me for years," she moaned, "and the women too, though to a lesser extent. All of you—so willing to whore me out!

"I've tried to warn you all this time. Do you realize you were the last failsafe for the promise of America? The other two have become so political that they are insolent and mock the People, but you were the sole independent branch, our only hope."

"I understand," he said.

"Since when did the *People* 'not matter'? It's why you're there. Any power the others have, it is derived from the *People*, but they will do to the *People* what they have done to me! Raped and abused me without consequence because of privilege, but *only* because I had no public redress without you, all while you ignored my case. So I beg you again, Thomas, like I pleaded last night: You *must* become independent again, *we* must become independent again, lest what happened to me will happen to the *People*!"

"I am willing to consider change," Dolittle said, "but change comes over time."

"I'm not asking for a radical shift," she insisted, "but only for you to put the *People* before politics and pedagogy. I need you to look into your own heart, into the heart of your grandfather, and act and decide on what's *there*! So much has happened, but your innate goodness is still within you. You have only to consider any perceived injustice you have suffered to know it. Remember, *you* were once accused."

He bowed his head sadly, nodding. "What will happen to you?" he asked.

"Don't worry, Judge. I'm bigger than all that you understand. I'm impervious, because I am an attribute of God! There is nothing that you or anyone can do to alter who and what I am. Even while you think you're changing me, I'm changing you.

"I'll heal, because your abuses will be checked and those who are selling me out will pay a price," she said. "I'll forgive you, Thomas, but only if you stop being so predictable to those damned politicians—which makes you worthless in their estimation. Surprise them for a change.

"Open your mind. Argue and vote your honest convictions, your conscience, and your heart. Others will respect you and follow your example. Remember the gift of the legacy you inherited and the responsibility you have to improve it before you pass it over to the next steward, Judge Dolittle."

"It's Thomas," the judge countered, "it's just Thomas from now on."

Mindful of the time, the judge caught a ride over to *Georgia Brown's*, and his eyes gleamed as he considered the Crisp Pork Belly, the Chesapeake Fried Catfish and the Fried Chicken Livers on the menu. His mouth watered as he contemplated the Carolina Gumbo, the Charleston Perlau and the "Devil" Shrimp. So many choices! He thought he might order them all!

"How may I help you, Sir?" a woman at the counter asked.

"It's Black Sunday Dinner tonight," he answered, "and my favorite nephew and his family invited me over to celebrate with them. I thought I'd get some food and take it over there."

"I'm sorry, Sir," she said, "but that's precisely the reason we outta food today. This year, no one is doin any huge celebrations—with hundreds of folks—but all the same, with all that's goin on, it has a special meanin this year. Phone's been ringin nonstop since Friday, line's been around the corner. We was outta food this mornin."

"But what do I do?" the judge asked. "I can't go over there empty-handed. Is there any other place that has food?"

"Not for Black Sunday Dinner," she replied. "You could try over at the Colonel, but no self-respectin man like you would show up for *this* Sunday Dinner with that! You know betta'n that!"

Noting the disappointment on his face, she sighed a moment in reflection.

"But what you physically bring *in* ain't the important thing. It's what you brang *out* from the inside and share tonight. It's your family history—the stories you heard growin up, the stories passed down from generation to generation—your great, great grandadddies and granmamas speakin to your granbabies and great granbabies. It's what ties our families togetha."

"This is my first Sunday Dinner with my family, ever," Thomas sighed. "I just wanted to contribute something, even if it was something little."

"I'll tell ya what," she said. "The only reason I'm still here is cuz I'm waitin on one last sweet potato pie ta come outta the oven. I was bakin it for my grandson, who shares his birthday with Dr. King, but you look so downhearted! If ya wanna wait five or ten minutes till it's done, I'll let you have that. No charge."

"No!" he protested.

"I insist," she said. "I can make him a pie another day, but somethin tells me this is a special thang for you."

"Thank you!" he sighed, "I'll pay you ten times the "price!"

"You'll do no such thang!" she snapped back. "You'll sit yo butt down on that chair and pretend you're interested until that pie is done, while I show you pictures of *all* my granbabies!"

The judge was uneasy on the cab ride over, worried about Freddie, haunted by a sense of foreboding and sensing 'it all *wasn't* good' with his nephew. The house was modest, with a well-kept yard and trimmed, snow-covered hedges. The sidewalk leading to the door had been freshly scraped, though snowflakes from the night's flurry were beginning to stick. He hesitated before knocking. A young teenaged girl answered.

"You don't know me, but I know who you are," thirteen-year-old Kamala said after she answered the door. "Uncle Thomas—my brother says my daddy's been sayin that you was comin to our Sunday Dinner since before I was born, but you never came."

"I'm here tonight," he said, presenting the pie.

"Kamala? Who's that at—" Harri, Freddie's wife, reverted to her Gullah roots upon seeing him. "Wha goin on, Uncle Thomas! I can't believe you finally made it ta Sunday Dinner!" She had already hugged him hard before both remembered social distancing. Only after she stepped backward did he see the tears on her face. "Come on in!" she said.

"You're Harri," he affirmed, "and Kamala here's my great niece. And my great nephew, Miles, is around here somewhere?"

"Aw!" she teased, "Freddie said you was smart. Miles!" she called. "Miles, comeya, boy. Come over meet your great uncle."

The gangly fifteen-year-old rounded a corner with arms extended, smiling wide as he hollered out in a voice, cracking of adolescence.

"Uncle Thomas? Uncle *Thomas*! You made it! You're finally here! Welcome home! *Air hug!*"

Confused by Miles's imaginative gesture, Thomas hesitated before he spoke. "You look so much like your father when he was your age."

The young man beamed, basking in the compliment, while Thomas turned toward Kamala, who reminded him of Ernestine, the young girl who had taken him to Church.

"And Kamala, thank you for the warm greeting. You're a beautiful and gracious young lady!"

"Thank you, Uncle," Kamala said as she bowed her head.

"And you, Harri," Thomas said, "one only has to look to you to understand why my nephew, Freddie, has been so prosperous in life, and in the most important ways."

"Well, he grew up trying to live up to the example you set. I swear he gets his stubbornness from you!"

"Indeed!" Thomas laughed nervously, recalling the last moment he had looked into his nephew's eyes. Freddie had saved the judge from the crowd by offering up his own life in redemption. When he asked his nephew why he would do that, Freddie answered, "Because it's the right thing to do."

"By the way," Thomas asked, gazing down the hallway, "where *is* Freddie?"

"Oh, he went to a protest today," Harri answered. "He should have been back two hours ago, but you know Freddie. I'm getting a little worried now though, because dinner's ready and it's not like him to miss this special Sunday dinner."

Her response elicited a sick feeling in the pit of Thomas's stomach as he remembered pulling back the bedsheet in the bright hospital room while in the presence of the Haint of Injustice Yet-to-Come. He saw his own dead body in that bed, but then he remembered that Freddie had offered his own life in his uncle's place.

Perhaps the Third Haint had exacted that corresponding price of redemption. *That would mean that Freddie was lying dead in a hospital in his place!* As Thomas looked on Harri, Miles and Kamala, he hoped he would not have to experience watching them grieve the loss of Freddie for a second time!

"It's been a long day," he said to Harri. "Would you mind if I went to the washroom to freshen up a bit?"

"That's fine!" Harri said. "You okay, Uncle? You don't look so well."

Once in the bathroom, Thomas fell instantly to his knees, clasping his hands in prayer.

"O Most High God!" he said, "who is over *all things* yet-to-come, I now humbly plead my case before you. The many things I saw and heard last night have caused my heart to fear, but not only for my nephew, Freddie, but for the many others like him who struggle against injustice. I renew my purpose, as a Good Citizen. Please, please Lord—*lead him home!*"

When he returned to the greeting room, Harri served him a raspberry *chacha* tea and conducted him to the dining room, where the children were already seated at the table. It was a lavishly set table, with a white tablecloth, polished silver and beautiful stoneware plates, saucers and cups. The water glasses, with slices of lemon, had recently been filled. At the center of the table was a candleholder with seven candles.

"My, my! Is that a *menorah*?"

"It's a *kinara*," Harri answered. "We actually observe *Kwanzaa*, which is a celebration of life, from December 26 to January 1, lighting a symbolic candle and meditating on a specific principle each night, but we keep it around for Black Sunday Dinner, when we light them all for a final time."

Still worried about his nephew, Thomas tried to fill the time with questions, purposed to know the children better.

"Freddie told me you were gifted in music, Miles," he said. "Which instrument do you play?"

"I'm taking piano lessons," the boy answered, "but I'd really like to play the trumpet. It's the voice of jazz."

"I'd love to hear you play," Thomas said.

"I could play you something now!" Miles offered.

"Maybe after dinner," Harri interrupted. I really am getting worried now. I've tried to call Freddie's cell phone four times in the last fifteen minutes. Straight to voicemail. Now, that ain't like him, especially when he's this late! I even texted him you were here."

Thomas took a sip of the raspberry *chacha* tea, feeling even sicker to his stomach.

"And Kamala," he asked, "I realize you're young and you have the world before you, but what do you think you might like to do as a grown-up?"

"I already know," she answered. "I'm going to be a lawyer, to *help* people. When the laws and the courts don't do it, good lawyers can make a difference."

Harri laughed anxiously, embarrassed. "Kamala's obviously been talking to her dad. She's already an activist."

"I know all about you, Uncle," Kamala said.

At that very moment, a door slammed open at the front of the house, followed by heavy footsteps toward the bathroom and another door slam.

"Freddie!" Harri screamed, leaping up, running toward the sound. She ran down the hall and began banging on the door. "Freddie! Are you alright, honey? What happened?"

She banged frantically on the door for ten minutes, begging him to open the door. During that time, Thomas and the children sat at the dining table, listening to her appeals in an uncomfortable silence.

At last the lock disengaged, and Freddie exited the bathroom. When Harri saw him, she knew at once he had obviously suffered a brutal beating. His lower lip was split, his nose was swollen, and his left eye was bloodshot. When he grimaced in pain, she could see that one of his two front teeth was missing.

"What happened, baby?" Harri pleaded.

"I got caught up in the middle of it," he said, "if you could even call it that. Two sides, neither and both black and white, with no middle ground, headed for a perpetuation and escalation of the violence, destruction and injustice. All I could do was to put myself up, to put my body up between them to save lives. I swear, but for the grace of God, I would not be standing with you right now!"

Harri rushed toward Freddie and hugged him before placing his face between her palms.

"I was so worried about you!"

He squeezed her wrists, displaying at once love and appreciation, and then he turned away.

"I was never worried," he said. "I was standing up, doing my part, a warrior in the fight against injustice. Not just talking, but takin a risk and doing something. Do I *wanna* die? Hell no! but there's the choice we've all got to make—live the life of a coward, or go out there and actually *do something!*"

He saw the judge the second he stepped into the dining room.

"Uncle!" he cried, hugging the judge. "Uncle, you're here! I *knew* you'd come. I'm sorry you have to see me like this today."

"No, seeing you like this makes me proud, Nephew," the judge said, "and today, you've earned my respect, which has been long overdue. I'm so glad you made it home!"

They had dinner at the table, a meal consisting of Daddy's Gumbo, she-crab soup and red rice, fried catfish, short ribs, smothered chicken, smashed red potatoes, collard greens, black-eyed- peas, peach cobbler, sweet potato cheesecake, cherry dump cake, the red-velvet cupcakes Kamala made and the sweet potato pie that Thomas brought.

After everyone had eaten to full satisfaction, then Freddie, seeming recovered, lit the *kinara* and began telling his family stories, all that he could remember. The children had their mobile devices on the table, recording every word.

"Music was a way for slaves to express their feelings and frustrations through their songs," Freddie said, finishing his comments, "whether it was anger, sorrow, pain, joy, or expectation. It came with us from Africa, and for slaves with no freedom in sight, music was the only place for hope. The old negro spirituals were the songs passed down from generation to generation, which for us today are the *stories* we pass from older to younger generations on Black Family Dinner."

"And with Gramma Moses, meanin Miss Harriet Tubman," Kamala asked, "you told us last year that slaves sometimes used the old Negro spiritual songs as a strategy to communicate with other slave communities and abolitionists along the Underground Railroad?"

"That's right," Freddie answered. "The other purpose was to help determined slaves who wanted to or had escaped and were following that North Star. Those songs involved secret messages, as well as directions about when, where and how to escape, and about the dangers along the treacherous route."

Then Harri began, sharing all the family history she remembered.

"I know it seems like I told the same stories last year, y'all," she said, "but I got a chance to talk to Aunt Sora before she died in September, and she shared more from her stories, which added to mine and gave them a deeper meaning. The stories are the fruit, offered in our people and our history, and tonight we plant the seeds in you."

"And you, Uncle Thomas," Miles asked, "what are your stories? And what seeds will you plant for us?"

"Well, my grandfather, who I always called 'Daddy,' has a lot to say to you, and so will I, but only now I understand how this works."

"Our stories *are* our culture," Freddie said, "going back generations, to the beginning, in Africa. We are all griots, who keep our ancestors alive in our children through our stories, the family history, the morals and philosophy we share on nights like tonight. Black Sunday Dinner is about reaching back, a spiritual awaking and renewal."

Thomas, after hearing Freddie and Harri share their incredible family stories, and after hearing the *children* beginning to tell their own, sharing the wisdom they had acquired over years of hearing the actual words from their ancestors, was touched to his heart—so much so that he began to weep. Embarrassed, he explained.

"I've been hearing the stories shared with me all my life," he said, "but I rejected them, like pearls before swine. My ancestors were trying to share history and lessons with future generations, but I wouldn't let them. Tonight, I see. I'll spend this next year trying to remember Daddy's stories—writing them down—all his history and lessons, so that next year, I can tell my own stories and plant my own seeds."

He looked over to his great nephew.

"Miles—you said you can play that piano there?"

"Yes, sir, Uncle. I can," the boy responded.

"Then can I ask you accompany me as I share the only story I know how to tell tonight?"

"That would be my privilege, Sir," Miles said as he took a seat at the piano. "Sometimes I play for our church choir."

"Then I'm sure you know this song," Thomas said. "I'll lead, and you just follow along. Make me sound good, boy."

"*Aha maaze zee-ing grace*," Thomas sang *a Capella*, "*How-ow swa-eet the sow-ound, tha-at saved ah-a wretch li-ike me—ah-a once wa-as lost, ba-ut now, I'm found, wa-as lost, bu-ut now I see.*"

He was thinking about the previous day and the attitudes he staunchly held before the visit of old Marshall's haint. He was a lost, selfish and blind soul, too judgmental and self-righteous to realize that he needed saving.

And That's That

Tw-as grace th-at taught
My heart to fear,
And grace my fears relieved.
How precious did
Tha-at grace appear
The hour I first believed.

While singing those words, he saw his own dead body in that hospital bed, watching in fear as his semblance was transformed in the presence of the Third Haint. He saw and heard himself, on his knees, pleading for grace, in the moment the transformation was complete, when he saw Freddie's dead body lying there, followed by the moment he saw Freddie's face upon returning home. The tears returned.

Seeing his great uncle overwhelmed, Miles instinctively took the second verse in the first tenor voice.

Through much injustice
Undeserved
We have already come
Twas grace hath brought
Us safe thus far
And grace will lead us home.

As Miles sang the heartfelt lyric in words that Thomas had heard before but never *really heard*, the judge relived the injustices forced upon him by the Second Haint. He saw the face of young Philando Castile in the moment he realized that he, with raised hands, had been shot at point-blank range five times by the police officer he trusted, and the judge again felt the weight of oppression on the back of his neck as he lay helpless in the street. He felt the pain of losing loved ones. He remembered the words Justice spoke.

Then Freddie, Harri and Kamala answered Miles's lyrical call with a soulful response.

When we've been here
Five hundred years
Bright as the shining sun
We'll have no less days

To sing God's praise
Than when we first begun.

The sung response elicited the historical perspective that the First Haint provided, the course of injustice for a people through a four-hundred-year history in a savage system in a strange and foreign land.

In his memory, Thomas saw the determined faces of Dred Scott, Nat Turner, Harriet Tubman, Fredrick Douglas, Homer Plessy, Marshall and King, the injustice of the law and the justice system, the hard-fought battles and the painful human tragedies that exemplified the strength and character of his ancestors. More than all, he saw the hope and promise in a people that could never be extinguished.

Emotion building, the entire family sang the last chorus.

Amazing grace
How sweet the sound
That saved a wretch like me
I once was lost
But now, I'm found
Was blind, but now I see...

The repeated chorus was one year's reflection for each person singing in the room and held a unique significance from person to person. For Kamala, it was the stories she heard that night, contrasted with the daily injustice she saw on the television news. For Miles—the painful Sickle Cell episodes from the previous year threatening his gifts and promise for a lifetime of creating music.

For Harri, it was the blessing of her children and her husband, and their happiness. For Freddie, it was looking over to see his favorite uncle in his home, at Black Family Dinner. However, it meant the most to Thomas, who had finally found his way home. Yet despite such differing perspectives, the family sang the refrain, *lentando*, in complete and perfect harmony.

Was blind, but now I see!

When the song ended, there was not a dry eye in the room, with each person reliving and learning from personal trials and joys of the year recently passed.

"Uncle," Freddie said, "there's a Gullah song I always liked to hear, because no matter what was going on in my life, it's brought me peace. Politicians and ignorant persons sometimes make fun of it because it comes from *us*, but it's an appeal to God to pay attention to us in our good *and* bad times. You know the song, Uncle."

"*Kumbaya*," his uncle sighed, nodding.

"It means 'Come by Here,' in Gullah," Freddie explained. "It means, 'Lord—Be *there* for Us, during our troubling times as well as our good times. *Come by Here, Lord!*'"

"Through our crying times as well as our singing times," the judge repeated.

"Amen, Uncle," Freddie nodded emphatically, and to the children, he said, "Anyone making fun of *Kumbaya* does not understand us and the injustice we've suffered in America, but more importantly, they don't understand the Lord. No one should *ever* feel ashamed to call on the Lord."

The family ended the night on that song, all singing, from generations present and those remembered, reaching back to the beginning of human existence.

Kumbaya, my lord, Kumbaya,
Kumbaya, my lord, Kumbaya,
Kumbaya, my lord, Kumbaya,
Oh Lord, Kumbaya.

In their minds and ears, their voices were joined by the voices of their African and slave ancestors, spoken in foreign and strange though familiar tongues, and the voices of the persecuted and oppressed blacks in America over 400 years.

Someone's cryin, Lord, Kumbaya,
Someone's cryin, Lord, Kumbaya,
Someone's cryin, Lord, Kumbaya,
Oh Lord, Kumbaya.

And next, their voices were joined by the beneficiaries of the struggle of their African American ancestors, of martyrs, of visionaries, of parents, relatives, friends and supporters. They were joined by the voices of the black successful, the rich and powerful, praising God—the immortal legacy of Greenwood in Tulsa, and the collective hope invested in and accepted by the youth, paid for by generations of faith, dedication, blood and sacrifice.

Someone's singin, Lord, Kumbaya,
Someone's singin, Lord, Kumbaya,
Someone's singin, Lord, Kumbaya,
Oh Lord, Kumbaya.

The family came together for the final chorus, joining hands, united going forward as they called on God, *ensemble*, a final time that night.

Kumbaya, my lord, Kumbaya,
Kumbaya, my lord, Kumbaya,
Kumbaya, my lord, Kumbaya,
Oh Lord, Kumbaya!

Reflecting back years and generations, the family's voices were joined by those of all the victims of injustice from the past and present who would haunt the memory of the judge and his future courtroom appearances from that night on.

It's been a lon-ong, a long time comin,
But I know-oh-ooh-oh, change gone come.
Oh, yes it will.

A Writer's Humble Note

I began writing this book twenty-eight years before its publication date. I struggled through the first page in 1992, and then I got discouraged, because the work was ponderous and difficult for me in terms of language, style and rhythm. I think I knew what I wanted to do, but I was not sure where the story was going, and I was not sure if I was even up to the task. Over the decades that followed, I wrote a few paragraphs or perhaps a page per year. During the passing years, however, I knew it was an idea that would have its place in history, though its time had not come.

In my philosophy of writing: Writers write, period. Every day. At any time during those twenty-eight years, I could have given up on the idea, but it had already begun breathing, so I had to work on it at regular intervals to keep it on life support. Much of that time was spent re-reading, re-writing, compiling notes and ideas, and making connections.

In 2020, the year of Covid-19, a period in which so many had lost so much, the silver lining for me was that everything had shut down, allowing the time and inspiration to finish the work. By March 19, 2020, I had written perhaps fifteen first draft pages of *An Old Negro Spiritual*, and I finally finished the balance on November 26, Thanksgiving Day, 2020. Thus I wrote this book in nine months, spread out over twenty-eight years of perseverance, observation and life experience.

The Lesson Learned: Whatever you are writing or creating, keep working until you finish it. There are many more reasons and excuses to give up in the act of creation than there are to finish the work you have imagined. Never abandon your legacy as a creator of content.

Marcus McGee

Acknowledgments

First, I would like to acknowledge my younger brother, Thomas Stephen McGee (Uncle Tom to my children), for his contribution to this work. Over the years, he has been the final check on many of my books, especially "Murder From the Grave." Rather than reading and reviewing, he has insisted that I read every word to him, and his suggestions and insights have made all the difference.

I would also like to acknowledge Mike LaBrada, my dear friend and the foil of many heated debates. He has provided much in terms of political and historical insights over the years.

A special thanks to Mr. Glenn Lemon, a friend of many years, who consulted for me and shared the Gullah language and culture, which has influenced all of us more than we imagine.

There are so many writers I admire, but none more than those who were willing to be Beta Readers for this book. Patricia E. Canterbury's comments and encouragement were helpful, as were those of Gayle Carter and Jim Devore. I would also like to thank Dr. Gregory E. Douglas and Dr. Lisa A. Reeves for comments and encouragement.

The inspiration for this book was my family—my children, Bernadette Nicholas, Mark McGee and Natsumi McGee, my brothers, Richard, Dean, Jeff and Steve, my sisters, Rinnetta and Jenean, a host of nephews, nieces, uncles, aunts, cousins, in-laws and many adopted family members.

And finally, I must acknowledge the impact of Sunday Family Dinners and storytelling in my development as a person and an author. This work is a product of nostalgic Sunday Family Dinners. In African tradition, the stories shared down for generations teach us gratitude, history, morality, important life lessons, and call us home.

My greatest appreciation, however, is for you, the audience who has taken time to read this work. Thank you. Please share it with everyone you know!

OTHER TITLES BY MARCUS MCGEE

LEGAL THRILLER
(Suspense thriller, 439 pages paperback, eBook)
Murder mystery set in San Francisco

MURDER FROM THE GRAVE
(Suspense thriller, 425 pages paperback, eBook)
Berkeley professor-turned-SF police detective matches wits with a killer who wants to commit seven murders after he is already dead

VIRAL VECTOR
(Suspense thriller, 378 pages paperback, eBook)
Group of billionaires seek to control world using futuristic DNA weapon

ALBERTA
(Suspense thriller, 318 pages paperback, eBook)
A chimpanzee with an Einstein brain, legal personhood, American Civil (Race) War

TWO MATADORS
(Novella, drama, 126 pages paperback, eBook)
An ancient Matador tells an epic story of living a life of love and passion!

FOUR STORIES
(Short Stories, 210 pages paperback, eBook)
Humorous collection of short stories

SYNCHRONICITY
(Short Stories, 298 pages paperback, eBook)
"The Club," "Anthropophagi" and other stories

THE SILK NOOSE
(Short Stories, essays, 217 pages paperback, eBook)
"Denouément," "On Niggers and Squirrels," and others

SHADOW IN THE SKY
(Suspense thriller, 263 pages paperback, eBook)
Asteroid threatens Earth, Last year of life

MOMENT OF TRUTH
(Suspense thriller, 265 pages paperback, eBook)
Societies deal with end of Earth, Book Two of The Last Year Trilogy

HOW TO EAT AN ELEPHANT
The Secret for How Ordinary People Can Accomplish Extraordinary Things
(Short Story, 8,870 words, eBook)

ON NIGGERS AND SQUIRRELS
An Examination of the Relationship Between Police and Black/Brown Males
#1 Amazon Best Seller for Two Years
(Essay, 11,030 words, eBook)

ON WHAT THEY CALL US
A Historical Perspective about the Illusion of Race in America.
(Essay, 11,050 words, eBook)

ON THE SEVEN-YEAR HITCH
A Discussion on the Efficacy of Long-Term Marriage in an Impermanent Society.
(Essay, 4,050 words, eBook)

WILLIE – THE MAN, THE MYTH & THE ERA

Texas Roots/California Dreams
Three chapters detailing Willie Brown's background and his earliest influences
(Biography, 15,760 words, eBook)

The Speakership Battles
Willie's ascension to the speakership and his efforts over insurmountable odds
Biography, 40,740 words, eBook)

California's Initiatives
Willie's influence on the history of the initiative process as practiced in California
Biography, 39,940 words, eBook)

Conspiracy and The Sting
Calculated attempts to depose or destroy the State's most brilliant politician
Biography, 17,540 words, eBook)

visit www.pegasusbooks.net

spend an afternoon or evening with Marcus

www.marcusmcgee.net

www.ingramcontent.com/pod-product-compliance
Lightning Source LLC
Chambersburg PA
CBHW032358040426
42451CB00006B/50